MW01295444

The Young Theologian's Handbook

Christian Doctrine

Darryl E. Riden

A division of Christ Powered Ministries

xulon
PRESS

Dedication

This book project is dedicated to my son, William Taylor, and my daughter, Caitlin Daryl. I am thankful that you both are *"young theologians"* and I'm amazed how God is already using you to proclaim His salvation and Word to this generation. I love you deeply and I can't imagine life without you.

In Memory of my mother, Alda Williams Riden. Mom no longer sees dimly, but now beholds the face of her Savior and Lord, Jesus Christ.

Thanks and acknowledgements

I am so very thankful that Jesus Christ loved us first. That He would save us and make us His own. My reason to live is to serve my Savior and King. I deserve nothing, but in Christ I have everything. Thank You Jesus!

I want to thank all of my youth group students through the years who have been so hungry for Truth and have allowed me to be a part of their discipleship process. Thanks especially to all the students that were a part of the Young Theologians Summer study groups in Kingsport, TN and the Journey students in Morristown, TN.

I am grateful to all our ministry partners who prayerfully and financially support CPM, and to my family for their great encouragement throughout the building of this ministry. Special thanks to Steve and Ginny Williams, Kevin and Brandy Spaugh, First Baptist Tellico Village Ladies Bible Class, Charlie and Teresa Barnard, Jason and Heather Russell, Mrs. Iva Crawford, Mrs. Myrtle Ledbetter, and Bill and Zula Riden, for their added assistance in bringing this book project to fruition.

I appreciate Taylor and Caiti's help with typing and proof-reading and their continuous excitement about this outreach project...even though they mock my typing abilities.

I am very thankful for all the Christ-centered pastors, student ministers, and lay leaders who daily work with young people on the "frontlines." You are my heroes. I hope in some small way this handbook will assist you in bringing the hope and truth of Jesus Christ to this generation.

I thank God for the great theologians and apologists He has used to bring so much depth and insight to the church body; many of whom are showcased within the quotes and historical figure sections of this book.

I am also very grateful for the amazing men and women of God throughout Church history who have stood on the verity of His Word and would not compromise their walk with Christ and the true doctrines of our Faith...even when it meant their certain death. The modern Church today owes these believers an enormous debt and honor. Not only the giants of our Faith, but also all the men and women leading ordinary, faithful lives throughout the centuries facing extreme difficulties and tribulation, but standing nonetheless. We will someday know their names too.

"All of life illustrates Biblical doctrine."
                                        -Dr. Donald Barnhouse

Preface

K arl Barth once said, *"In the Church of Jesus Christ there can and should be no non-theologians."* I believe this is a fair statement. The main reason I put this theology handbook together is to provide at least a starting point for young people to better comprehend historic Christianity. This is by no means an exhaustive overview of Christian theology. It is simply a primer for students to focus on the basic tenets of our faith and have a fuller understanding of Christianity so they can *"contend earnestly for the faith which was once for all delivered to the saints"* (Jude v. 3).

There is a great need in this day to get back to the foundations of Christianity. *Theology is the study of God.* It is the purpose of this book to educate students in doctrinal positions of historic Christianity and how these doctrines point to the truth, love and salvation of Jesus Christ.

In an age of experiential religious pursuits, theology can be seen as a hindrance to "feeling" where God is leading the Church. Experience is never to be the foundation for theology, but rather sound theology should be the foundation for our experience. C.S. Lewis said, *"If you do not listen to theology, that will not mean you have no ideas of God, but it will mean you will have a lot of wrong ones."* We need to be certain we are worshiping the God revealed in Holy Scripture and not a god of our own making.

It is vital that as Christians we understand why we believe what we say we believe in. In my three decades of student ministry I have seen methods and philosophies of ministry towards youth outreach and discipleship shift and change drastically. The most troubling shift has been the current lack of doctrinal instruction. This doctrinal vacuum along with the intense attacks against Christianity and the authority of the Bible have crippled many of our American churches and the confidence of today's young believers.

In many churches basic theology has been replaced by a felt-need approach to youth ministry. Many student ministries have a "babysitting" mentality that devolves into playing games, having a snack, and telling a short story. We often know much more about the main speaker, or a musician, than we know about Jesus and His Word at the end of our church and youth services. It is a common misconception that young people will not "sit still" to hear quality Bible teaching. This leads to the false assumption that they must be entertained to get them to participate in a local church fellowship. We neglect sound theology at our own peril.

The abandonment of absolute truth in our postmodern culture has certainly helped to produce a weak, confused and fickle faith in this generation of young believers. With the onslaught of cultic and heretical teaching we are seeing much misinformation regarding, and wrong understanding of, the most basic doctrines of Christianity. This attack on pre-suppositional truth has invaded the soul of a generation that now views Christianity with skepticism and suspicion. We must realize that this is a spiritually hungry generation and they will believe in something, right or wrong. It is our task as the Church to offer them the concrete Truth of Jesus Christ. Not only is Christianity built upon faith, it is also built upon *facts.* *"Therefore whoever hears these sayings of Mine, and does them, I will liken him to a wise man who built his house on the rock."* (Matt. 7:24)

It is always an exciting moment when we see the light come on in a young person's eyes when they realize the Bible is God's *living Word,* and He still speaks powerfully through it to us today. It is the impact of solid Bible teaching and a caring, loving Christ centered fellowship that brings hope and direction to students today. They are starving for the truth. We must stand in the gap for them and make sure they have strong biblical teaching that confronts and challenges them with the truth claims of Christ, and after conversion, gives them a solid foundation of biblical discipleship to build their lives upon. The way we think directly affects the way we live, and thus for young people to truly live for Christ they must have a correct Biblical worldview. How can we know how to live as Christians if we do not study God's Word?

So many of our churches are declining and dying because young people and young adults no longer attend. Current polls taken by Barna Research, Pew, Time, and others show that a majority of Christian, church-attending young people in America will leave the church by their late teens to early twenties. This should be an alarming statistic to church leaders. Sadly, most churches do not have to read professional polling data to be shocked into reality. All they have to do is look at their weekly congregation and see that few young adults are walking through the church doors.

For the most part, young people are not attending because they see the church as irrelevant and the Bible as antiquated and hard to understand. It is time to educate our Christian students in core doctrines of the Faith and why they need to understand Christian theology more fully. When Christian students dig deep into the truth of our Faith they begin to come alive. It is amazing how the Word transforms the human heart and sets it on fire. Line by line, truth by truth. This awakening of the young person's heart by the Word will also awaken our churches as these young people become vibrant members of growing local fellowships.

How tragic that we often see young people walk away from our churches because they are disillusioned and disinterested. The teaching of the Word of God should never be a dull, lifeless experience. It is a privilege to read and study the Word and we have the promise that it will never be an empty pursuit (Isaiah 55:11). It will certainly make a difference when students attempt to defend their faith in Christ.

Correct theology brings us into a correct understanding of who the Person of Christ is, and through the study of God's Word we will see Him as the only hope of salvation and all truth. I Timothy 4:16 states, *"Take heed to yourself and to the doctrine. Continue in them and you will save both yourself and those who hear you."* It is crucial that our theology is sound when proclaiming Christ through preaching, teaching, counseling, church planting and evangelism.

If we are to carry forth the Word of Life we need to know that same Word intimately and correctly. We should always be ready to give an answer for the Hope we have in us (I Peter 3:15). It is important that young people understand that theology is not just a "church" thing but is actually vital to their everyday walk and growth in Christ.

My prayer is that we as Christian ministers, teachers, parents, grandparents, and mentors will pour our lives into the young people we encounter and proclaim Jesus as the Way, the Truth, and the Life...that He is the only way to the Father. Letting them know that when they accept Jesus Christ as Lord and Savior they are a part of something much greater than themselves... they become the Church.

I hope this handbook will also be a helpful tool to young believers who are witnessing to their peers and families. Your passion and focus to reach out to others is a great encouragement to the Body of Christ, young and old. Remember, Jesus loves you more than you can imagine...stand on His Word, trust Him with everything, He has you covered!

Praying for you,

Darryl

Contents

John 14: 6

<u>Subjects</u>:

Angels

Focus verse:

B *ut the angel answered and said to the women, "Do not be afraid, for I know that you seek Jesus who was crucified. He is not here; for He is risen, as He said. Come see the place where the Lord lay."*

-Matthew 28:5-6

Greek: *Angelos* (ang'-el-os) a messenger, an angel.

Theological note:

An angel is a spiritual being, created by God, who has the duty to carry out God's will, praising the Godhead, and guarding the throne of God. Angels are not to be worshiped or exalted by man. Angels are not needed as agents of revelation and are never to be seen as god-like or "lesser gods." All angels are subject to Jesus Christ.

Pastoral quote:

"Angels are spirit's, but it is not because they are spirits that they are angels. They become angels when they are sent. For the name "angel" refers to their office, not their

nature. You ask the name of this nature, it is spirit, you ask it's office, it is that of an angel, which is a messenger."

-Saint Augustine

Reference verses:

Likewise, I say to you, there is joy in the presence of the angels of God over one sinner who repents.

-Luke 15:10

When the Son of Man comes in His glory, and all the holy angels with Him, then He will sit on the throne of His glory.

-Matthew 25:31

Hebrews 1:1-9   I Thessalonians 4:16
Acts 5:19   Psalm 91:11   Colossians 2:18
Galatians 1:8

Quote:

"The angels will know their Master's property. They know each saint, for they were present at his birthday."

-C.H. Spurgeon

Commentary:

There has been an explosion of interest in angels in our generation. They are seen as saviors, revealers of deeper truth, beings worthy of worship, prophetic ancient "spirit guides," and even extraterrestrials that will lead Man to redemption and hope. These are all distorted and dangerous views of angelic beings. Angels are no longer needed as agents of divine revelation because we have the authoritative Word of God revealed in Scripture. They also are not needed as an intermediary messenger between God and believers because of the indwelling of the Holy Spirit within all born again Christians.

When we search the Bible for the truth about angels we have a clear idea of what they are and why they were created, even though Biblical information about the nature of angels is limited. We know they have free will, as evidenced by a third of them choosing to rebel with Lucifer. We also find that an angel is a special class of created spiritual being, intelligent, full of strength, and not bound by natural law. They were created all at one time at some point in the creative order before man (Psalm 148), and their numbers are innumerable.

There are many examples of angels performing specific tasks in the Old Testament. These tasks basically include protection, proclamation, and punishment. We find in the New Testament that angels are used by the Lord mainly for proclamation. The Book of Revelation reveals that angels will have a prominent role during the Tribulation Period. The Bible implies in certain passages that the angelic host ("*army*") has a distinct order and rank. The term "archangel" implies that there are angels that have command over ranks of other angels for the purpose of carrying out the will of God.

References to the Seraphim and Cherubim (Ezekiel ch.1 and Isaiah ch.6) reveal these beings to be special orders of angels that attend to the Throne of God. They are also the only angels that are described as having wings. All other Biblical angelic appearances describe angels as having the form of men, men clothed in white garments, and occasionally men accompanied by a brilliant white light or fire. None are described as female or in the form of a child.

The concept of humans having a personal "guardian angel" is not supported by Scripture, but the Bible does support that God will dispatch an angel(s) to physically help believers for a specific task or bring momentary protection.

The idea that when "good" people die they become angels in Heaven is a common misconception of the origin of angels and is certainly not found in the Bible. We are never to place our trust in the power of angels or attempt to contact them. Angels of God will *not* allow humans to worship them (Rev. 19:10).

In I Peter chapter 1 we read, *"...those who have preached the Gospel to you by the Holy Spirit sent from Heaven—things which angels desire to look into."* Angels are intensely aware of Jesus' redemptive work at Calvary. They looked on as He paid the sin debt for mankind on the cross. An angel removed the stone from the tomb where Jesus lay, and angels proclaimed to His followers that He had risen from the dead (Matt. 28:1-8). Angels marvel at Salvation, for they will never fully understand what it means to be lost in sin and then placed in the redemptive righteousness of Jesus Christ. Even so, they rejoice when people call on the name of the Lord, repent and are saved (Luke 15:10).

The angelic host is loyal to God and will not act against His will or speak contrary to His Word. Ultimately they were created to serve and worship God, proclaiming Christ's glory and majesty to all creation at the will of the Godhead.

And suddenly there was with the angel a multitude of the heavenly host praising God and saying: "Glory to God in the highest, and peace and goodwill toward men!"
-Luke 2:13-14

Historical Figure: *Francis Schaeffer*

Francis August Schaeffer was an evangelical theologian, philosopher, and Presbyterian pastor. He was born January 30, 1912 in Germantown, Pennsylvania. Strongly opposed to Theological Modernism (Liberalism) he supported a more traditional Protestant faith and a pre-suppositional approach to Christian apologetics. His writings greatly influenced his generation and his impact is still felt today. Schaeffer established the *L'Abri* community in Switzerland for the purpose of teaching young people theology and apologetics. Some of his most popular books were, *"How Should We Then Live?"* *"The Christian Manifesto,"* *"The God Who Is There,"* and *"Escape From Reason."* He died in 1984.

Term: *"Etymology,"* studying the true meaning and values of words. How words are derived.

Hymn: *"Angels We Have Heard On High"*
      Words: Traditional French carol, 1862
      Music: *GLORIA*, traditional French carol.

Angels we have heard on high,
sweetly singing o'er the plains;
And the mountains in reply,
echoing their joyous strains.
Gloria in excelsis Deo!
Gloria in excelsis Deo!

Baptism

Focus Verse:

*T**here is one body and one Spirit just as you were called in one hope of your calling; One Lord, one faith, one baptism; One God and Father of all, who is above all and through all, and in you all.*

-Ephesians 4: 4-6

Greek: *Baptizo* (bap-tid'-zo) immerse, to submerge, to baptize

Theological note:

Baptism is an ordinance of the Lord Jesus, obligatory on every believer, where he is immersed in water in the name of the Father, the Son and the Holy Spirit, as an outward sign of his fellowship with the death and resurrection of Christ, of remissions of sins, and of repentance and walking in the newness of life.

Pastoral Quote:

"We may never be martyrs but we can die to self, to sin, to the world, to our plans and ambitions. That is the

significance of baptism; We died with Christ, and rose to new life."

-Dr. Vance Havner
American pastor, author
(1901-1986)

Reference Verses:

For by one Spirit we are all baptized into one body- whether Jews or Greeks, whether slaves or free, and have all been made to drink into one Spirit.

-I Corinthians 12:13

Do you not know that as many of us as were baptized into Christ Jesus were baptized into His death? Therefore we were buried with Him through baptism into death, that just as Christ was raised from the dead by the glory of the Father, even so we also should walk in newness of life.

-Romans 6: 3-4

Luke 3:21   Colossians 2:12   I Peter 3:21   Acts 18:8

Quote:

"Baptism is simply a testimony- the first public profession of faith that the believer makes. The rite shows the community that the individual is now identified with Christ. It is a symbol of an inward reality."

-H. Wayne House
American seminary
professor, author

Commentary:

Baptism is one of the two ordinances (also known as sacraments) of the Christian Church, the other being the *Lord's*

Supper. We see clearly in the book of *Acts* this process: The Gospel is proclaimed, The Holy Spirit brings conviction of sin, people repent of sin, by faith they receive Christ, forgiveness and salvation are given, and the redeemed person follows up with a public baptism. Historically when a person receives Christ he or she follows the conversion event with *water baptism.* This is *not* a part of the regenerative salvation experience. It is not required for salvation (example: the thief on the cross).

There is some confusion within the Christian community about the subject of baptism so we must begin with Scripture and end with Scripture to find the truth. The term *baptism* in the Bible does not always mean *water* baptism. In Mark 10:37-38 and Luke 12:50 Jesus speaks to the baptism of suffering He would endure on the cross and asks His disciples, *"Are you able to be baptized with the baptism I experience?"*

In Mark 1:8 John the Baptist says, *"I baptize you with water, but He (Jesus) will baptize you with the Holy Spirit."* Water is not the focus here. Instead it is a spiritual baptism that takes place at salvation. In Acts 1:5 at *Pentecost* the believers in Christ are gathered and the Holy Spirit fills them. They receive the Holy Spirit and He is poured out on them. I Corinthians 12 provides a picture of spiritual baptism in Christ. We are all baptized into *one Body* with many gifts.

At the moment of your salvation you are baptized with the Holy Spirit and receive all of the Holy Spirit you will ever have. There is no "second blessing" of the Spirit imparted at baptism. There is no relationship between water baptism and being filled with the Holy Spirit. There is no Scriptural directive that would support the idea of "baptismal regeneration" (the belief that water baptism has saving power).

Jesus was baptized, not to be filled with the Spirit and be saved, but for God to bear witness to the world that Jesus was the Christ (John 1:32-33). We are to follow through with water baptism using Christ as our example (Matthew 3:16 and Acts 8:36). Baptism is also a *symbol* that we are *"clothed with Christ,"* (Galatians 3:27) and *"buried with Him in baptism..."* (Colossians 2:12).

Peter's first sermon in the 2nd chapter of Acts is often used as a proof text that you must be baptized to be saved. *"Repent and each one of you be baptized in the name of Jesus Christ for forgiveness of your sins, and you will receive the gift of the Holy Spirit."* Remember, we must study the Word in <u>context</u>. What is Peter saying? In Acts 3:19 Peter says, *"Therefore, repent and turn back so that your sins may be wiped away."* He does not mention baptism. In I Peter 3:21 he clarifies by using the Ark of Noah as an illustration of God's saving grace. *"And this pre-figured baptism, which now saves you- not the washing off of physical dirt but the pledge of a good conscience to God- through the resurrection of Jesus Christ."* Notice Peter says, *"...not the washing off of dirt..."* Peter is stating that it is *not* water baptism that saves you, but it is *what* baptism <u>represents</u>, which is our *faith* in the risen <u>Christ</u>, that saves us.

Paul stated in I Corinthians 1:17, *"For Christ did not send me to baptize, but to preach the Gospel."* In this verse Paul separates the salvation experience and baptism. Paul was the greatest missionary in history. If baptism is essential to salvation then Paul's ministry could actually be seen as a failure because historically he rarely baptized converts after he preached (I Cor. 1:14-17).

In the *Great Commission* (Matthew 28:19) Jesus commands us to *"...make <u>disciples</u> of all nations, baptizing them in the name of the Father, Son, and Holy Spirit."* Disciples are believers, followers of Christ. We first lead people to Christ and after they <u>*believe*</u> on His name we are then to <u>*baptize*</u> them. If baptism saves, Jesus would have said to go into the world and *baptize* people and *make* them disciples.

It is not Jesus *and* baptism that saves us. Baptism is simply a public declaration that a believer has confessed Jesus as Lord (doctrine of the *Believer's Baptism*). They have been set free by the blood of Christ, redeemed, washed from sin and now identified with Jesus' death, burial and resurrection. We are making a public statement that we now belong to Jesus Christ. It is an outward sign of our union with Christ and a way of publicly marking a new way of living our life, now identified as a Christian.

We need to also understand that throughout Church history a public declaration of Christ could bring persecution and death from hostile forces. To be publicly baptized was no small thing. Even today a public commitment by new believers in Jesus Christ can bring intense persecution, death, harassment, and isolation in many countries. These persecuted believers making this very real stand for Jesus today is a powerful witness and an amazing encouragement to all believers throughout the world.

If you are saved but not yet baptized, talk with a church leader or minister and let them know your desire to follow through with this powerful congregational experience and ordinance of the Church.

<u>Historical Figure</u>: *Isaac Newton*

Sir Isaac Newton was born on January 4, 1643 at Woolsthorpe Manor, in Lincolnshire and died on March 31, 1727. He was an English physicist, mathematician, astronomer, philosopher, alchemist, and theologian and ranked by Britain's *Royal Society* as the most influential scientist in history. His book *Philosophiae Naturalis Principia Mathematica* (1687) described the Three Laws of Motion and universal gravitation which was instrumental in advancing the scientific revolution. Newton was also a devout Christian. He produced more work on Biblical hermeneutics than the natural science he is most widely remembered for today. In all of his scientific studies he clearly saw God as the Creator who brought forth the majesty of the created universe.

Term: *"Pentateuch,"* The first 5 books of the Old Testament. Commonly called *The Law.* Also the *Torah*, Hebrew for *law*; authored by Moses.

Hymn: *"Just As I Am"*
Lyrics: Charlotte Elliott, 1834
Music: *"Woodsworth,"* William B. Bradbury, 1849

Just as I am without one plea,
that Thy blood was shed for me,
and that Thou bidd'st me come to Thee,
O Lamb of God, I come, I come.

The Church

Focus verse:

A *nd to make all see what is the fellowship of the mystery, which from the beginning of the ages has been hidden in God who created all things through Jesus Christ; to the intent that now the manifold wisdom of God might be made known by the Church to principalities and powers in the heavenly places.*

-Ephesians 3:9-10

Greek: *Ekklesia* (ek-klay-see'-ah) a calling out, church, an assembly of believers

Theological note:
　　The Lord Jesus is the Head of the Church, which is composed of all His true disciples, and in Him is invested supremely all power for its government. According to His commandment Christians are to associate themselves into particular societies or churches, and to each of these churches He hath given needful authority for administrating that order, discipline, and worship which He hath appointed. The regular officers of a church are bishops, elders, and deacons.
　　　　　　　-Southern Baptist Theological Seminary 1858

Pastoral Quote:

"The Church is a hospital for sinners, not a museum for saints."

-Vance Havner

Reference verses:

So continuing daily with one accord in the temple, and breaking bread from house to house, they ate their food with gladness and simplicity of heart, praising God and having favor with all the people. And the Lord added to the Church daily those who were being saved.

-Acts 2:46-47

That He might present her to Himself a glorious Church, not having a spot or wrinkle or any such thing, but that she should be holy and without blemish.

-Ephesians 5:27

Revelation 21:9   Colossians 1:24   I Timothy 3:15
Revelation 22:17

Quote:

One hundred religious persons knit into a unity by careful organizations do not constitute a church any more than eleven dead men make a football team. The first requisite is life, always.

-Aiden Wilson (A.W.) Tozer
American pastor, author
(1897-1963)

Commentary:

The *Church* is the family of God. The *Ekklesia*, the *"called out ones."* Those who have placed their faith in Christ as Savior are members of the true church. The primary characteristic of the church in the New Testament is devotion and allegiance to Jesus Christ who established the Church under His authority (Matt.16:13-20). The Church began at *Pentecost* with the coming of the Holy Spirit (Acts ch.1- 2).

Jesus said *"...on this Rock I will build my Church"* (Matt.16:18). This was not implying that He would build the church on Peter's authority. He was stating that He (*Jesus*) was the Rock, the foundation, and that the proclamation of the *Gospel* (by Peter and the Apostles) was how the Church would be built. Jesus is the Head of the Church (Eph.1:22-23).

Today many people have the mistaken notion that the church is a building where people gather and do "religious" things. The reality is that Christians *are* the Church because they are the dwelling place of the Holy Spirit on earth (Rom. 8:9). The earthly church is called the *church militant*. Those believers who have passed away and are now in Heaven are called the *church triumphant*. We are also called the *Body of Christ* and the *Bride of Christ*. It is within the reality and context of the church that God reveals Himself in the world and the Gospel of Jesus Christ is proclaimed.

The church is a single worshiping fellowship permanently gathered in the true sanctuary which is the Heavenly Jerusalem (Gal.4:26, Heb.12: 22-24). The Church was not established to be a nation on earth; we are to be a People among the nations. The church is *one* but is made up of many different fellowships and denominations worldwide. It is holy, universal, and its mission is to worship and proclaim Christ in every generation and nation. Prayer, preaching the Gospel, and the ordinances of baptism and the Lord's Supper are some of the main features of local congregations.

Attending a Bible believing fellowship should never be seen as an option because the Church is also a *local body of believers*. We must encourage and love one another as we, by our very showing up week after week, proclaim that Jesus Christ is alive in the world today. Our consistent involvement with a local fellowship of believers is the most powerful ongoing public witness we have that we are followers of Jesus Christ. Christians who say they do not need to attend church have missed this major point. They have slipped into wrong thinking. This attitude is selfish and uncaring because the local fellowship is not just about an individual but about the whole Body.

Another way to look at this is to see it from God's view. He has given us everything in Jesus and He loves the Church. When we walk away from a local fellowship we are saying we do not love what God loves the most. When we have a true thirst for Christ we will want to be with His people. It is not about gathering with "perfect" people. It is about being with family (through good times and bad), encouraging one another, standing together for a cause much greater than ourselves, and reaching out to our communities with the hope and Gospel of Jesus Christ.

The Church is made up of Christians with various spiritual gifts and abilities. You are needed in your church because you bring things to the Body that no one else can. You also need the gifts and encouragement of other believers to help you grow, mature and produce ministry. As Christians we are called to love one another, which is hard to do when we are not a part of a local fellowship. The modern day version of the isolated, non-participating Christian is not scriptural, along with the idea that only church staff should do the work of the church and the congregation just needs to attend services.

Local churches can have severe problems, mismanagement, confusion, and disunity. There certainly can be nonbelievers portraying themselves as Christians who are not saved but act religious. There can also be those in attendance who knowingly cause division and disruption. God knows His Church and He will separate the saved from the unsaved in time (Matt. 13:24-30). Our response to a dysfunctional local fellowship (no local church is perfect) is to keep our eyes on Jesus and worship Him above all else. Never let a person distract you from the real reason we come together as believers.

If you allow people to cause you to avoid or depart from a local fellowship you are letting them dictate your relationship with Christ. Fellowship does not have to be as hard as we sometimes make it. Always seek peace with one another when that is possible. If a church is teaching falsehood, or centered around personalities and their human efforts, talents, and ambition, you certainly have the right to leave and find a balanced Bible-believing, Christ-centered fellowship to attend, but never leave angry or arrogantly.

Our place in the fellowship is to walk in the Holy Spirit and exhibit the fruit of the Spirit (Galatians 5:22-26). If you are involved in a Bible teaching, Christ exalting church you should plant yourself there and bloom. Today many believers jump from one church to another and never become a productive, accountable member of the local body. In the long run they are robbing themselves of the great blessing of building ministry shoulder to shoulder with other believers.

The New Testament outline for church organization is straightforward and brilliant in its simplicity. Every member is gifted for service and ministry, then utilized in cooperation with other members for the good of the whole Body (Romans 12:1-8 and I Cor. 12:12-31). Specific tasks of the local church are met by designated persons for the daily functioning of the body. These are pastors, elders, teachers, deacons, evangelists, and bishops. The local church is always to be led by the Holy Spirit and structured in a way to fulfill the Great

Commission (Matt. 28:18-20). Evangelism and missions are the lifeblood of the Church. When we stop reaching out with the Gospel we stagnate and implode.

The Church, the Mystery of the Fellowship, is a profound reality that ushers us into a glorious Christ exalting fellowship. It is a privilege and a blessing to be called the children of God and to proclaim His Word on earth (Gal. 4:6-7).

Behold what manner of love the Father has bestowed on us, that we should be called children of God! Therefore the world does not know us, because it did not know Him. Beloved, now we are children of God; and it has not yet been revealed what we shall be, but we know that when He is revealed, we shall be like Him, for we shall see Him as He is. And everyone who has this hope in Him purifies himself, just as He is pure.

-I John 3:1-3

Historical Figure: *John Wycliffe*

John Wycliffe was born c.1320's in England. He was a brilliant theologian, preacher, Bible translator, and reformist. He was an early dissident in the Roman Catholic Church, and his followers were called *Lollards*. The Lollard Movement was actually a precursor to the Protestant Reformation which came 200 years later. He was an early advocate for translating the Bible into English and eventually produced a handwritten copy called *The Wycliffe Bible* in 1382 A.D. His passion to get the Bible into the hands of common people greatly influenced other men like Luther and Tyndale. He is seen as one of the most prominent figures in church history. Wycliffe died in 1384.

Term: *"Ecumenicalism,"* doctrines and practices of the "ecumenical movement" among Protestant groups since the 1800's with the goal of achieving universal Christian unity;

often compromising or distorting key doctrinal issues to obtain that goal.

Hymn: *"Blest Be The Tie"*
      Words: John Fawcett,1782
      Music: Johann G. Nageli,
      arranged, Lowell Mason, 1845

Blest be the tie that binds
our hearts in Christian love;
The fellowship of kindred
minds is like to that above.
Before our Father's throne
We pour our ardent prayers;
Our fears, our hopes, our aims are one,
our comforts and our cares.

Creation

<u>Focus Verse:</u>

*I*n the beginning God created the Heavens and the Earth.

-Genesis 1:1

<u>Greek:</u> *Ktisis* (ktis'-is) the act of creating, the ongoing creative act, original formation

<u>Theological Note:</u>

God did not create the world and the universe out of pre-existing materials. He spoke into being the heavens and the earth which literally did not exist before. Because God is perfect His creation was also originally perfect and essentially good. Nature is dependent upon God for its existence and continuance. It is able to progress even in a fallen state because of its divine design, autonomy and integrity. Ultimately all creation is for the glory and purpose of God.

<u>Pastoral Quote:</u>

"Some people, in order to discover God, read books. But there is a great book: the very appearance of created things. Look above you! Look below you! Read it. God,

whom you want to discover, never wrote that Book with ink. Instead He set before your eyes the things that He made. Can you ask for a louder voice than that?"

-Saint Augustine

Reference verses:

Thus says God the Lord, who created the Heavens and stretched them out, who spread forth the Earth and that which comes from it.

-Isaiah 42:5

Has thou not known? Has thou not heard, that the ever-lasting God, the Lord, the Creator of the ends of the earth, faints not, neither is He weary? There is no searching of His understanding.

-Isaiah 40:28

Matthew 25:34   John 1:1-3   Romans 1:20
Romans 8:22   Genesis 1:27

Quote:

"Any error about creation also leads to an error about God."

-Thomas Aquinas (1225-1274)
Italian theologian, priest
and philosopher

Commentary:

"Creatio Ex Nihilo," creation out of nothing, is a central teaching of the early church fathers such as Irenaeus and Augustine of Hippo. This truth revealed from the Word of God was in direct opposition to Greek philosophical arguments that stated the world and cosmos were eternal, having

no beginning or end. The early church fathers proclaimed *Ex Nihilo* as a biblical doctrine and in doing so proclaimed the awesome reality of God's power and transcendence. They also acknowledge the pre-eminent role of Jesus, the *Logos*, in the creative process. John 1:3 boldly states that Jesus Christ, *the Word* (John1:14), created all things, and that He is the giver and sustainer of life.

John Calvin agreed with Augustine and Aquinas that creation reveals the knowledge, creativity, and wisdom of God. Believers understand that creation has been corrupted by sin and awaits a glorious restoration by Christ the Lord. It is interesting that many current secular scientists who have promoted evolutionary views of the cosmos are questioning their previous beliefs, now stating that the Biblical account of creation is more compatible with what they actually observe in nature.

The Bible is clear that God is the Creator of all things and everything belongs to Him. As humans we have been given dominion over the earthly creation and even in a fallen world system we are ultimately accountable to God for what we do with His creation (Gen.1:26-28). Even in its fallen state creation is brilliant, profoundly beautiful, and mysterious. The Bible says that all creation declares God's glory and that man is without excuse if they deny His existence (Rom. 8: 20-21). Scripture also reveals that God will one day restore all of creation to its original glory and perfection.

For the earnest expectation of the creation eagerly waits for the revealing of the sons of God. For the creation was subjected to futility, not willingly, but because of Him who subjected it in hope; because the creation itself also will be delivered from the bondage of corruption into the glorious liberty of the children of God. For we know that the whole creation groans and labors with birth pangs together until now.

-Romans 8:19-22

Historical Figure: *Martin Luther*

Martin Luther was born in Eisleben, Germany on November 10, 1483. He was a German monk, theologian, university professor, and the man God used as the catalyst for the Protestant Reformation. Luther's theology challenged the role of the Pope by saying that the Bible is the true and only infallible source of religious authority. Luther's *95 Theses* nailed to the Wittenburg door was the turning point that began the Reformation Period. He also made the Bible available to the common people of his day by translating the *Latin Vulgate* into German, enabling them to understand the Word of God instead of going through the hierarchy of the Catholic Church. This act influenced other prominent Bible translations and the future 1611 *King James Bible*. As a prolific songwriter, Luther's hymns inspired the development of congregational singing. He set a model of practice for a clergyman to be married. His impact was felt throughout the Christian world. Luther died on February 18, 1546.

Term: *"Ecclesiology,"* the study of the historic Christian Church, its practices, order, structure, and authority.

Hymn: *"How Great Thou Art"*
> Words: Carl Boberg, 1886-translated Stuart Hine, 1949
> Music: Swedish Folk Medley-Arr. Stuart Hine, 1949

O Lord my God! When I in awesome wonder
Consider all the worlds Thy hands have made,
I see the stars, I hear the rolling thunder,
Thy power throughout the universe displayed,
Then sings my soul, my Savior God to Thee;
How great Thou art, how great Thou art!
Then sings my soul, my Savior God to Thee;
How great Thou art, how great Thou art!

The Cross of Christ

Focus verse:

L *ooking unto Jesus, the Author and Finisher of our Faith, who for the joy that was set before Him endured the cross, despising the shame, and has sat down at the right hand of the throne of God.*

-Hebrews 12:2

Greek: *Stauros* (stow-ros') a stake or cross set upright, an instrument of capitol punishment and torment

Theological note:

In Jesus' death on the cross God placed the death consequences of sin for all humanity upon the Son. Adam, by his sin, plunged all of humanity into spiritual death constituting them sinners and condemned to eternal punishment. Jesus, the incarnated, sinless, Son of God, vicariously and substitutionally paid man's penalty for sin, thus providing the way for all mankind to be reconciled to a Holy God and obtain eternal life.

Pastoral Quote:

"To abandon all, to strip one's self of all, in order to seek and follow Jesus Christ naked to Bethlehem where He was born, naked to the hall where He was scourged, and naked to Calvary where He died on the cross, is so great a mystery that neither the thing nor the knowledge of it, is given to any but through faith in the Son of God."

-John Wesley

Reference verses:

For the message of the cross is foolishness to those who are perishing, but to us who are being saved it is the power of God.

-I Corinthians 1:18

There were also two others, criminals, led with Him to be put to death. And when they had come to the place called Calvary, there they crucified Him, and the criminals, one on the right hand and the other on the left. Then Jesus said, "Father, forgive them, for they do not know what they do."

-Luke 23:32-34

Colossians 2:14-15   John 19:17   Ephesians 2:16
Colossians 1:20

Quote:

"Men have said that the cross of Christ was not a heroic thing, but I want to tell you that the cross of Jesus Christ has put more heroism in the souls of men than any other event in human history."

-John Graham Lake
businessman, evangelist
(1870-1935)

"Cursed be all teaching and learning that is not subservient to the cross of Christ."

-Jonathan Witherspoon
Scottish born, Presbyterian minister,
President of New Jersey College (Princeton),
Signer of the Declaration of Independence.
(1723-1794)

Commentary:

The preaching of the cross is at the very heart of Christianity. The sacrifice of the sinless Son of God, spilling His blood for man's redemption is the central theme of the Gospel. *"Without the shedding of blood there is no remission of sins"* (Heb.9:22).

The cross was an instrument of immense torture and shame. The Romans were experts in execution, public humiliation and torture, the cross being their ultimate punishment for enemies of the state. The English word, "excruciating," is derived from the Latin, *"ex crux,"* meaning *"out of the cross."* Jesus' ordeal on the cross was bloody, brutal, and agonizing. He literally took upon Himself the sin of the world. No human words could ever describe what He actually went through as our substitute.

In the midst of devastating agony Jesus cried out to God, *"Father, forgive them, for they know not what they do."* This plea to the Father revealed the heart of Jesus, for He came to seek and to save that which was lost, willingly laying down His life for us. *"And being found in appearance as a man, He humbled Himself and became obedient to the point of death, even the death of the cross"* (Philippians 2:8).

In studying the Old Testament we have a solid foundation for understanding the concept of sacrifice and redemption. When the New Testament speaks to these issues we see the profound connection revealed in Christ. It is Calvary that opens our eyes to just how much God detests sin, and how much He truly loves us. Paul says he would only *boast in the cross of Christ* because he knew that is where our redemption was purchased by the precious blood of Jesus (Gal. 6:14).

In Isaiah chapter 53 we see a clear picture of Jesus, the Suffering Servant, the Lamb of God (John 1:29), slain before the foundation of the world. Isaiah's description of the coming Messiah was prophesied more than *700 years before* Jesus was born. *"He was wounded for our transgressions, He was bruised for our iniquities; the chastisement for our peace was upon Him, and by His stripes we are healed."* Jesus came to die on the cross at a specific time in history for the redemption of man.

The cross of Christ is significant because it is there that we find forgiveness, hope and rescue. The shape of the cross is an enduring symbol of historic Christianity and was first used in various forms in the ancient church to identify true believers. What was once a symbol of torture and dread is now a universal symbol of hope and forgiveness.

We, as Christians, are called to pick up our cross and follow Him. This means we are to put to death our fleshly desires and ambitions and seek the will of God for our lives. When people saw a condemned man carrying his cross to the site of execution they knew he was never coming back. In like manner we as Christians have died to our old life, never to return. Now a new creation, we are filled with the Holy Spirit, led by His presence, putting away sinful lusts and selfish pursuits. When we live with this sacrificial mindset and empowered by the Holy Spirit, we are capable of living a life that would be impossible otherwise. We are now placed in the position to faithfully follow Christ and worship the Lord in Spirit and in Truth.

Above all, the cross was central to God's salvation plan for fallen man. Before the foundation of the world Jesus was prepared to lay down His life for you and me. Because of God's enormous grace we *"...who were once far off have been brought near by the blood of Christ"* (Eph. 2:13). God's love is truly amazing!

"And you being dead in your trespasses and the uncircumcision of your flesh, He has made alive together with Him, having forgiven you all trespasses, having wiped out the handwriting requirements that was against us, which was contrary to us. And He has taken it out of the way, having nailed it to the cross. Having disarmed principalities and powers, He made a public spectacle of them, triumphing over them in it."

-Colossians 2:13-15

Historical Figure: *The Apostle John*

John, son of Zebedee and the brother of James, was one of the original twelve apostles of Jesus. He was a young fisherman when Christ called him to be His disciple. He and his brother James were called the *"sons of thunder."* Tradition says that John was the first cousin of Jesus. He is the author of these New Testament books: the *Book of John, I, II, III John*, and *Revelation*. He was one of the first apostles to run towards the tomb after the Resurrection, and the only apostle to follow Jesus all the way to the Cross. John lived to be around 95 years of age and is said to have been martyred. He is greatly revered through the centuries for his steadfast love for the Savior, his place as an early church father, and his contribution to the canon of Holy Scripture.

Term: *"Orthodox,"* Belief in the standards of accepted and true doctrines taught in the Bible.

Hymn: *"The Old Rugged Cross"*
        Words and Music: George Bennard, 1913

On a hill far away stood an old rugged cross
the emblem of suffering and shame;
and I love that old cross where the dearest and best
for a world of lost sinners was slain.
So I'll cherish the old rugged cross,
til' my trophies at last I lay down;
I will cling to the old rugged cross,
and exchange it someday for a crown.

Death

Focus verse:

*T*herefore, just as through one man sin entered the
world, and death through sin, and thus death spread
to all men, because all sinned.

-Romans 5:12

Greek: *Thanatos* (than'-at-os) death, something deadly

Theological note:

There are two Biblical uses for the word death: The ces-
sation of life, and for those who are lost without Christ. In
regards to the unbeliever, death is the separation from God
because of their sin. The Fall of Man ushered in sin to God's
perfect creation and thus brought the curse of death to the
created order. Death will be destroyed when Jesus Christ
returns and establishes His Kingdom on earth.

Pastoral quote:

*"Death may be the king of terrors, but Jesus is the King
of kings!"*

-D.L. Moody

Reference verses:

Yea though I walk through the valley of the shadow of death, I will fear no evil; for You are with me; Your rod and Your staff, they comfort me.

-Psalm 23:4

O death, where is your sting? O Hell, where is your victory? The sting of death is sin, and the strength of sin is the law. But thanks be to God, who gives us the victory through our Lord Jesus Christ.

-I Corinthians 15:55-56

Hebrews 9:27   Colossians 2:12-15   Psalm 56:13
John 5:24   Revelation 21:4

Quote:

"And come He slow or come He fast, It is but Death who comes at last."

-Sir Walter Scott
Scottish novelist, poet
(1771-1832)

Commentary:
Death is brutal. Death is darkness. Because of Adam's sin and the resulting fall of humanity we are under the curse of death. The Bible is clear that sin leads to death: physical, emotional and spiritual. We see the effects all around us, it is man's greatest fear, and it seems so final and devastating. If you have ever stood over the grave of someone you loved you understand the stark, painful reality of passing, fragile life.

Death will not have the final say in creation and in humanity, for Jesus has conquered death by bringing the hope and surety of eternal life to those called by His name. Even the created order will be restored when Christ reigns over the earth.

Our lives often seem to be one loss after another but we must put our faith and trust in the One who walked out of a tomb, never to die again, resurrected to new life and holding the promise of eternal peace and joy. *Love has killed this brutal darkness.* We can now live our lives without this suffocating fear. If you are saved by the blood of Christ you may die once but you will certainly live again. As the apostle Paul stated, *"To live is Christ, to die is gain!"* (Phil. 1:21)

D.L. Moody once said, *"Someday they will say that Dwight L. Moody has died but the truth is I will then be more alive than I ever have been. Do not mourn for me for I will be with Jesus!"*

The idea that the dead can exist on earth as ghosts is simply false. When we die there are only two options for humanity: Heaven or Hell. Those who are born again, who have placed their faith in Jesus Christ, will enter Heaven. Those who have rejected Christ will be bound in Hell to face the second death.

As Christians we may walk through the *shadow of the valley of death* but we will not stay there. When we follow Jesus we pass from death to life. How awesome the power of God, how magnificent is the love of Christ!

"For the wages of sin is death, but the gift of God is eternal life in Christ Jesus our Lord."

-Romans 6:23

Historical Figure: *Stephen*

Stephen was one of the very first ordained deacons of the early Church. He was set apart by the Apostles because of his love for Christ and his servant heart (Acts 6: 1-7). He was stoned to death by the Jewish council in Jerusalem after testifying to the validity of Jesus Christ and His resurrection. He is regarded as the first Christian martyr.

Stephen's name is significant to Christians today because of the courageous stand he took for Christ. At his stoning he fell to his knees and cried out, *"Lord do not hold this sin against them."* Saul, who later became the apostle Paul, was the one who approved and oversaw Stephen's death.

Term: *"Heresy,"* a doctrine (teaching) that deviates from the established truth of God's Word. A false teaching.

Hymn: *"Blessed Assurance, Jesus Is Mine"*
       Words: Fanny J. Crosby, 1873
       Music: Phoebe P. Knapp, 1873

Blessed assurance, Jesus is mine,
Oh what a foretaste of glory divine!
Heir of salvation, purchase of God,
born of His Spirit, washed in His blood.
This is my story, this is my song,
Praising my Savior all the day long;
This is my story, this is my song,
Praising my Savior all the day long.

The Devil and Fallen Angels

Focus verse:

S *o the great dragon was cast out, that serpent of old,*
called the Devil and Satan, who deceives the whole
world; he was cast to the earth, and his angels were cast
out with him.

-Revelation 12:9

Greek: *Diabolos* (dee-ab'-ol-os) false accuser, devil,
slanderer
Satanas (sat-an-as') Satan, the accuser

Theological note:
Satan, the Devil, is a created angelic being who rebelled
against the Godhead and convinced one-third of the angelic
hosts to rise up against the authority of God. Because of this
rebellion God cast them out of Heaven. Satan is called by the
Bible the *father of lies* and a *murderer from the beginning.*
He is the author of evil, the tempter of man, and the accuser
of the Church. His kingdom is spiritual and is located above
the earth. Fallen angels are called demons and do the will of
their master the Devil. Satan is under the sovereignty and
rule of God and has been defeated at the Cross of Christ.

Pastoral quote:

"What can you do against Satan? Do nothing but this: cry to his Master against him. He may be mighty, but set the Almighty One upon him. He who accuses you, refer him to your Advocate when he brings your sin before you, throw the blood of Atonement in his face."

-C.H. Spurgeon

Reference verses:

Be sober, be vigilant; because your adversary the Devil walks about like a roaring lion, seeking whom he may devour. Resist him, steadfast in the Faith, knowing that these same sufferings are experienced by your Brotherhood in the world.

-I Peter 5:8-9

Then He will also say to those on the left hand, "Depart from Me, you cursed, into the everlasting fire prepared for the Devil and his angels."

-Matthew 25:41

Ephesians 6:10-18　　John 12:31　　I John 3:8
Colossians 2:15

Quote:

"The Devil will let a preacher prepare a sermon if it will keep him from preparing himself."

-Vance Havner

Commentary:

There has been considerable confusion and misinformation regarding Satan and demons. The Bible makes clear that the Devil is not the "opposite" of God. He does not reign in Hell. He is not all powerful and equal with God. He is not a god. He is not the spiritual brother of Jesus. He is not red and does not have horns, a tail, or a pitchfork! So who is he?

Lucifer was an archangel created by God who had close access to the Throne of God. Because he was created with freewill (as we are), he made the choice to rebel against his Creator and began his perverted quest to be worshipped as God. Pride was his great sin (Isaiah 14:12-14, the five *"I Will's"* of Satan). During the Heavenly rebellion Lucifer convinced a third of the angels to follow him and they (now known as *demons*) are under his command. At the climax of the heavenly rebellion Lucifer and his angels were cast out of Heaven. He then became known as the Devil and Satan. He is identified as the serpent in the Garden who deceived Eve. When Adam also succumbed to Satan's temptation, man was plunged into sin and death, which is known as The Fall of Man.

Satan is full of fury, perversion, malice and cruelty. He is the father of lies and the original murderer. Satan imitates, he never creates. He is the master counterfeiter. All falsehood and evil began with him, and his anger is directed toward God and God's creation. Satan's great desire was to destroy man's redemption but he was defeated at the cross of Jesus and there Christ triumphed over him (Col. 2:15). Because he is defeated he knows his time is short and has implemented an all out assault on mankind, and specifically the Body of Christ.

The Devil and demons are under the sovereignty of God and are a part of God's overall plan for creation. He has allowed the Devil a finite amount of time and then He will banish Satan and every demon to torment in everlasting fire (Rev. 20:10). *Hell was created originally for these rebellious angels, not humans.*

Satan is stronger and more cunning than human beings and he is the ultimate deceiver. We as Christians should be aware of his existence and power but should never cower in terror before him and demonic beings. *A Christian cannot be possessed by demons because we are the possession of Christ and filled with the Holy Spirit.* But a Christian can be manipulated and hindered in their walk with Christ if they allow satanic influences into their lives. Demons can possess *unbelievers.* Demons can harass, cause trouble, confusion, and prompt wicked behavior. They can also appear as "familiar" spirits (in the likeness of a dead loved one, historical figure, etc.) to deceive those susceptible to "haunting" delusions. Satan and demons do not have the power to kill, for only God has the power over life and death, but they can instigate murderous rage and murderous thoughts in humans.

We should understand that Satan can come as an *"angel of light"* (II Cor. 11:14) and deceive people into believing his counsel is from God, beneficial and harmless, when in reality his objective is to bring devastation and shame to all people including Christians. The Devil rarely comes in horrifying forms, he would rather seduce than scare. Satan hates the Word of God and continues his strategy of casting doubt on the Bible's veracity and inspiration. He wants you to doubt God so that even as a Christian your life will not produce fruit for the Kingdom of God. He successfully used this strategy with Adam and Eve in the Garden, and he even attempted to subvert Scripture with Jesus in the wilderness temptation (Matt. 4:1-11). Another strategy of the Devil today is to perpetuate the lie that he *does not* exist and that evil is merely a psychological manifestation.

He is the tempter and will try to get us involved in ungodly behavior, pursuits, and thoughts. The occult, new age, astrology, alcohol and drug abuse, sexual sin, and occult based entertainment (movies, books, music, websites, games) are powerful gateways that can draw even Christians into satanic compromise or bondage. *Satan always attacks your thought life first.* He is patient, he does not care how long it takes you to compromise your Christian witness he just wants it compromised.

Satan craves even now to be worshiped. The reality is that if we are not worshiping Jesus Christ we are worshiping false gods/religions that originated with satanic deception and influence. He desires to keep humanity in spiritual death. The Apostle John described him as the *prince,* or *ruler,* of this world because mankind desires to stay in darkness (John 12:31). Stating further that *"...the whole world lies under the sway of the wicked one"* (I John 5:19). The Bible is clear that in this fallen world system Satan is an active force to bring spiritual harm. Satan is the one who has empowered the many antichrists (*anti,* meaning, *against*) present in every generation, and ultimately the Devil will give the actual Antichrist immense world authority during the Great Tribulation to bring spiritual devastation to the earth (Revelation Chapter 13).

As Christians we are always to test the spiritual content of everything we see, hear, and do in this world to discern whether it is of God or the Devil (I John 4:1). The Biblical definition of a false prophet or an antichrist spirit is this: *"Every spirit that does not confess that Jesus Christ has come in the flesh is not of God. And this is the spirit of the Antichrist, which you heard was coming, and is now already in the world"* (I John 4:2-3). Any teaching that denies that Jesus Christ is Lord and Savior is false.

As Christians we realize we are in a battle against evil principalities (read Ephesians chapter 6). We must seek wisdom from God to see satanic strategies and traps, and stand on God's Word to gain victory from demonic opposition. Always lift up the *Sword of the Spirit* (The Bible) as your main weapon in the midst of demonic oppression. Speak the Word!

As Christians we are never instructed to *run* from the Devil (James 4:7). We are called to put on the *"full armor of God"* and *stand* and resist him. In doing so, the devil will flee from our presence because of the power of the Holy Spirit and our faith in Christ. We have the promise of God that if we yield to the Holy Spirit within us that we will never be tempted beyond what we can stand (I Corinthians 10:13). As Christians we have the authority to cast out demonic spirits in Jesus' Name. Ultimately, Jesus will crush Satan's kingdom. *"For this purpose the Son of God was manifested, that He might destroy the works of the devil"* (I John 3:8b).

We as believers understand that this present world system is passing away and Satan will be banished forever (I John 2:17). Satan and demons are *not* omnipotent, omniscient, or omnipresent. Satan is a powerful opponent, but Jesus Christ is All-Powerful. Stand!

"You are of God, little children, and have overcome them, because He who is in you is greater than he that is in the world."

-I John 4:4

<u>Historical Figure:</u> *Myles Coverdale*

Coverdale was born *ca.*1488 in Richmondshire, England. He studied at Cambridge and eventually became a Lutheran pastor. He was a 16th century Bible translator who produced the first complete printed translation of the Bible into English. Coverdale was a loyal disciple of William Tyndale and assisted him in his translation work. He also superintended the publishing of King Henry VIII's *"Great Bible."* He was an important figure in the Protestant Reformation.

<u>Term:</u> *"Dualism,"* the concept that the world is controlled by two opposing, yet equal forces, good and evil, God and Satan. This idea denies the sovereignty and omnipotence of God.

Hymn: *"A Mighty Fortress is our God"*
>   Words: Martin Luther, 1529- translated, Fuderick
>   Hodge, 1853
>   Music: *"Ein'Festeburg,"* Martin Luther 1529

A mighty fortress is our God,
A bulwark never failing;
Our helper He, amid the flood
of mortal prevailing;
For still our ancient foe,
doth seek to work us woe;
His craft and power are great,
and armed with cruel hate,
on earth is not his equal.

Discipleship

Focus verse:

*T**hen Jesus said to His disciples, "If anyone desires to follow after Me, let him deny himself, and take up his cross, and follow Me."*

-Matthew 16:24

<u>**Greek**</u>: *Mathetes* (math-ay-tes') a disciple, a pupil, one who learns

Theological note:

Christian discipleship is following the Person of Jesus Christ. Adhering to the teaching and disciplines of the Faith found in the Holy Bible and giving one's full allegiance and obedience to Christ the Lord. Discipleship is the process of following Jesus and becoming mature believers instructed by Scripture and then instructing others to observe all that Christ commanded (Matthew 28:18). Our word *discipline* comes from the Latin, *"disco,"* which means to learn or get to know something or someone.

Pastoral Quote:

"It costs nothing to come to Christ, it costs something to follow Christ, it costs everything to serve Christ."

Dr. M. R. De Haan
American medical doctor
and pastor (1891-1965)

Reference verses:

Then He said to them, "follow Me and I will make you fishers of men." They immediately left their nets and followed after Him.

-Matthew 4:19-20

By this all will know that you are My disciples, if you have love for one another.

-John 13:35

John 8: 31-32   Mark 3:13-19   Luke 14: 25-27

Quote:

"When Christ calls a man, He bids him come and die."
-Dietrich Bonhoeffer
German pastor, theologian
(1906-1945)

"...allowing not a bit of the old life to be left; but only simple perfect trust in God, such trust that we no longer want God's blessings, but only want Himself. Have we come to the place where God can withdraw His blessings and it does not affect our trust in Him?"

-Oswald Chambers
Scottish pastor, theologian

Author, *"My Utmost For His Highest"*
(1874-1917)

Commentary:

When we follow Jesus and build our lives on His Word, He teaches and disciplines us to be obedient servants of God. This always results in a life that is pleasing to Him. Does this life of discipleship cost anything? Yes it does. It may cost us everything. People who say that Christianity is a "crutch" or a "feel good" religion do not have a full understanding of what it means to follow Jesus. To truly pick up our cross and follow Him means our self centered earthly ambitions and dreams must fade, now being replaced by a desire to live according to God's Word and the leading of the Holy Spirit within us.

As we trust and follow God's will He provides us with the desires of our heart that first please Him, and in turn, fuels the plans that He has redeemed us to accomplish. No longer do we seek the praise of people, for this is a prison of its own, but pleasing God is our highest aim. We must also be careful in what catches our attention. Many times the "shiny things" in the world capture us and we begin to drift away from this path of righteousness.

There are always believers who seek to "radically" follow Christ, as they look to the extreme to express their devotion to God. This can take different forms and mean different things to each of us. I would suggest that the most radical follower will always be the person who chooses to trust the Lord at His Word and truly live it out without compromise. That alone will make you very different in any generation. After all, "radical" actually means getting to the root or foundation of something.

We do not have the natural capacity within us to live the Christian life. People who think discipleship is "acting like" Jesus are mistaken. The Christian life *is* Jesus. Paul speaks to this when he said we are *"...always carrying about in the body the dying of the Lord Jesus, that the life of Jesus may also be manifested in our body"* (II Cor. 4:10). Being a disciple of Jesus is more than just having religious knowledge and performing religious rituals or good works. True Christianity is Jesus living *in* us, and working *through* us. *Christianity is not a religion, it is a relationship.* Religion is man's futile attempt to get to God, Christianity is God's path to reach and save man. This understanding of the Christian faith is foundational and transforming.

For the most part the process of discipleship unfolds within the context and care of the local church and by immersing ourselves in the Word (Romans 12:2). As we grow and mature we are then called to disciple others. Discipleship is a tremendous undertaking that culminates in becoming a mature, passionate Christian who is being transformed into the likeness of Jesus Christ (II Corinthians 3:18). You can trust God with your life and your journey of discipleship. He loves you more than you can imagine!

"I do not pray that You should take them out of the world, but that You should keep them from the evil one. They are not of the world, just as I am not of the world. Sanctify them by Your truth. Your Word is truth. As You have sent Me into the world, I also have sent them into the world."

-John 17:15-18

Historical Figure: *William Wilberforce*

William Wilberforce was born on August 24, 1759 in Hull and died on July 29, 1833. He was a British politician, a philanthropist and a leader of the movement to abolish slave trade. In 1785 he became an evangelical Christian resulting in major changes to his lifestyle and a lifelong commitment for reforming British politics. He headed the Parliamentary action against the British slave trade until *The Slave Trade*

Act in 1807. Wilberforce felt strongly about the importance of religion, morality, and education. Wilberforce supported the action for the complete abolition of slavery even after resigning from Parliament because of sickness. He died three days after hearing that the Slavery Abolition Act of 1833 had passed and became law. He was buried in Westminster Abbey, close to his friend William Pitt. Wilberforce's life has been an enormous inspiration for many generations of Christian's seeking justice for the poor, enslaved, and underprivileged.

Term: *"Meditation,"* to contemplate, to think deeply. Seeking the overall principle, truth, warning, exhortation or promise in a certain passage of Scripture. Biblical meditation is never the "emptying" of the mind, but instead it is the filling of the mind with God's Word.

Hymn: *"Stand Up, Stand Up For Jesus"*
    Lyrics: George Duffield, Jr., 1858
    Music: Adam Geibl, 1901

Stand up, stand up for Jesus, Ye soldiers of the cross;
Lift high the royal banner, it must not suffer loss:
From victory unto victory His army shall He lead,
Till every foe is vanquished, and Christ is Lord indeed!

Faith

Focus Verse:

*N**ow faith is the substance of things hoped for, the evidence of things not seen.*

–Hebrews 11:1

Greek: *Pistis* (pis'-tis) persuasion, conviction of the truthfulness of God, reliance upon Christ for salvation

Theological note:

Saving faith is the belief, on God's authority, of whatsoever is revealed in His Word concerning Christ; accepting and resting upon Him alone for justification and eternal life. It is wrought in the heart by the Holy Spirit and is accompanied by saving grace and leads to a life of holiness. Faith is a primary concept of Christianity. Without faith in Jesus Christ alone for salvation one cannot be a Christian.

Pastoral quote:

"Faith is a firm and sure knowledge of the divine favor towards us, founded on the truth of a free promise in Christ and revealed to our minds and sealed in our hearts by the Holy Spirit."

-John Calvin
French theologian
(1509-1564)

Reference Verses:

I have been crucified with Christ and it is no longer I who live, but Christ lives in me; and the life I now live in the flesh I live by faith in the Son of God, who loved me and gave Himself for me.

-Galatians 2:20

So then, just as you received Christ Jesus as Lord, continue to live in Him rooted and built up in Him, strengthened in the faith as you were taught and overflowing with thankfulness.

-Colossians 2:6-7

Hebrews 12:1-2   I Corinthians 16:13   Mark 11:22-23
James 1:5-6 Galatians 5:22

Quote:

"Faith in the Bible is faith in God against everything that contradicts Him-I will remain true to God's character whatever He may do. 'Though He slay me, I will trust Him'- this is the most sublime utterance of faith in the whole of the Bible."

-Oswald Chambers

"I don't understand all there is to know about the plan of salvation, but I don't understand all there is to know about electricity either, but I don't plan on sitting in the dark until I do."

-Vance Havner

Commentary:

Faith is the instrument by which a person is saved. We are justified before God by faith and by faith we live out our relationship with Christ (Romans 3:26). Jesus is the very real evidence of things not yet seen. Why? Because Christ has risen from the dead and in doing so has prepared the way for all believers to enter Heaven and enjoy eternal life in Him. Even though we do not see Heaven in this earthly life we are in fact citizens now if we are in Christ (Phil. 3:20-21).

Faith is an active confidence in God. Not ethereal wishful thinking but belief in the truth of Jesus Christ, the object of our faith. Faith is a response directed toward an object and defined by what is believed. *Faith is only as good as its object.* You can have faith that an old chair will hold you up as you are seated. When the chair breaks and you hit the floor you realize your faith in its stability was betrayed. Spiritually, the *object* of our faith must always be the sure foundation of the Person of Jesus Christ.

Historical Christianity is very different than all other religious systems of the past and present. All other world religions ask you to perform works, rituals, or meet man-made requirements and rules to achieve a reward. At the end of your life you may, or may not, go to "heaven" or some type of paradise, as the supreme deity decides your fate according to how you performed during your earthly exis-tence. Hinduism, for example, claims you are perpetually reincarnated to various forms of life until you reach spiritual perfection. This may mean you come back as a worm, an animal, beggar, etc. time after time. These religious systems offer no guarantee or hope of being loved by the specified deity or obtaining eternal life after death. Faith in false religions produces hopelessness.

With Christianity our salvation is settled at the *beginning*, not the end. Because of our faith in Christ we are immediately placed in a permanent, loving, righteous relationship with God. There is no question what will happen to us when we die. We are not bound by guilt, ritual, fear and disillusionment because we know that at death Heaven is our eternal home and no power on earth can stop us from entering into the presence, peace, and security of Jesus our Lord and Savior.

When we are saved we place our faith in the lordship and power of Jesus. **"We walk by faith, not by sight"** (II Cor.5:7). This means we have placed our full trust and belief in Christ and now our relationship to Him determines our priorities. This belief in Jesus removes our sin and also shifts our allegiances from worldly ambitions and relationships to Christ alone. Our faith in God will change our standards and convictions. It should always inform every area of our lives.

Daily faith is obedience to God's Word no matter what the circumstances of life are. Many Christians seem to be practical atheists because they say they believe the Bible but they choose not to obey the Word. I have heard it said, *"You only believe the parts of the Bible that you live."* In our pursuit of holiness and living a faithful life we must obey the Word. If God says do it, *do it*. If God says don't do it, *don't do it*. When we blatantly sin and walk away from righteous living we are in reality saying we have little or no faith in the instructions and promises of God (James 1:22).

Spurgeon said, *"When you can't trace God's hand, trust His heart."* Sometimes we do not see God working in our lives. We can feel isolated, fearful, and anxious. This is when walking by faith is crucial. Ultimately we know that God is far ahead of us in every circumstance and that He is fully capable of rescue, comfort and provision. Jesus is mighty to save and He is our solid, unshakeable object of faith.

How do we get to this place of complete trust? The same way you do with anyone else you learn to trust; you spend time with them, you speak to them daily, you share your real fears, hopes, dreams, failures, and joy. Jesus is patiently and lovingly drawing us to Himself. *He is with you and will never leave you or forsake you.* You can trust Him with your whole life and Jesus will never betray your faith in Him. Put your faith in the only One who is worthy of that trust. You will never regret giving everything to Christ.

"For whatever is born of God overcomes the world. And this is the victory that has overcome the world...our faith."

-I John 5:4

Historical Figure: *Apostle Paul*

Paul was a Jew and a Roman citizen who called himself "The Apostle to the Gentiles." He was one of the greatest Christian missionaries the world has ever known. Paul was saved as he was traveling on the road to Damascus. There he encountered the resurrected Jesus. Temporarily blinded and humbled he soon received the Gospel of Christ. He was then set apart by Jesus to take the Gospel to the Gentile world.

He wrote 14 books of the Bible through the inspiration of the Holy Spirit. These books are believed to be the earliest written books of the New Testament. Paul's influence on Christian thinking and doctrine has been profound. By God's grace, a man who once persecuted Christians became arguably the most influential minister in Christian history.

Term: *"Septuagint,"* The oldest Greek translation of the Old Testament. Latin for *seventy*, alluding to the 70 scholars that worked on this translation of the Bible. Also known as the *LXX*.

Hymn: *"My Faith Has Found A Resting Place"*
Lyrics: Lidie H. Edmunds, 19th C
Music: *Landas*, Norwegian Folk Melody
arranged by William J. Kirkpatrick

My faith has found a resting place,
not in device or creed;
I trust the Ever living One,
His wounds for me shall plead.
I need no other argument,
I need no other plea,
It is enough that Jesus died,
and that He died for me.

Glorification of Believers

Focus verse:

*S*o *also is the resurrection of the dead. It is sown in corruption, it is raised in incorruption; it is sown in dishonor, it is raised in glory; it is sown in weakness, it is raised in power. It is sown a natural body, it is raised a spiritual body.*

-I Corinthians 15:42-44a

Greek: *Aphthartos* (af'-thar-tos) immortal, non-decaying, incorruptible

Theological note:

The bodies of men after death return to dust, but their spirits return immediately to God: the righteous to rest with Him, the wicked to be reserved under darkness to the judgment. At the last day, the bodies of all the dead, both just and unjust, will be raised.

-Southern Baptist Theological Seminary, 1858

Pastoral quote:

"But courage, believer! Your body shall rise again. Laid in the earth it may be, but kept in the earth it cannot be; the

voice of nature bids you die, but the voice of the Omnipotent bids you live again!"

-Charles Haddon Spurgeon

Reference verses:

And if Christ is not risen, your faith is futile; you are still in your sins! Then also those who have fallen asleep in Christ have perished. If in this life only we have hope in Christ, we are of all men the most pitiable.

-I Corinthians 15:17-19

Moreover whom He predestined, these He also called; whom He called, these He also justified; and whom He justified, these He also glorified.

-Romans 8:30

II Corinthians 5:1-5   I Corinthians 15:50-54
I Thessalonians 4:13-18   I Corinthians 13:12

Quote:

"He is no fool who gives what he cannot keep to gain what he cannot lose."

-Jim Elliott
martyred American missionary
to Ecuador (1927-1956)

Commentary:

There are only two things in this life that will last for eternity: The Word of God and people. There are only two kinds of people: Those who are saved and those who are lost. The doctrine of Glorification teaches that those who are saved because of their faith in Christ will die only once and then be raised to new life. Those who are lost will face the *second death* (Revelation 21:8).

The Apostle John tells us that when Christ returns *"...we shall be like Him, because we shall see Him just as He is"* (I John 3:2). The good news of Christianity is that our resurrected bodies will be like Jesus' resurrected body, immune to decay, sickness and death. Jesus was raised in the same body that He died in, and in like manner we will be raised in our present likeness. All mortal bodies of Believers throughout history, though corrupted by the scourge of death, will be raised to new life, transformed into imperishable bodies, perfect and immortal. God will deliver us to a sinless, unblemished state.

The Apostle Paul compares the death of our earthly vessel to a seed sown in the ground. A seed is dead when planted but in the time of harvest it produces life. The harvest always produces abundantly more than the original seed contained. This is why he said we cannot conceive of what is waiting for us in Heaven and the glory of being raised in the likeness of Christ (I Cor. 2:9).

Glorification is the final step in the plan of redemption. The glorification of the Christian believer is the final fruit of salvation and the blessed and eternal state of the redeemed. *"For our citizenship is in Heaven, from which we eagerly wait for the Savior, the Lord Jesus Christ, who will transform our lowly body that it may be conformed to His glorious body..."* (Phil. 3:20-21).

We will someday be raised in power and glory because Jesus has conquered the grave. The burdens and pain of this earthly mortal existence will be over. The presence of sin will be terminated, and the sanctification process will be completed. Because of this truth you will see your deceased Christian loved ones again in Heaven and enjoy perfect communion with all believers and God eternally.

The profound truth of this doctrine is that Jesus is coming back to receive us to Himself, to change us gloriously, and that we are literally God's children. This truth should encourage and inspire us as it has millions of believers throughout history.

"But as many received Him, to them He gave the right to become children of God, even to those who believe in His name, who were born, not of blood, nor of the will of the flesh nor of the will of man, but of God."

-John 1:12-13

Historical Figure: *H.A. Ironside*

Henry Allen "Harry" Ironside was born on October 14, 1876 in Toronto, Canada. He was a Bible teacher, preacher, pastor, and author. Ironside was inspired by D.L. Moody after hearing him preach as a teenager. With only an 8th grade education, Ironside eventually became one of the greatest preachers and Bible teachers in the past century. He was a guest lecturer at Dallas Theological Seminary, traveled worldwide as an evangelist, and for a while was the pastor of Moody Bible Church in Chicago. Wheaton College presented him with an honorary doctorate in 1930. H.A. Ironside died in 1951.

Term: *"Eschatology,"* the study of end times, and Christ's Second Coming, according to Holy Scripture.

Hymn: *"Crown Him With Many Crowns"*
Words: Matthew Bridges, 1851
Music: *"DIADEMATA,"* George J. Elvery, 1868

Crown Him with many crowns, The Lamb upon His throne;
Hark! How heavenly anthem drowns all music but it's own;
Awake, my soul, and sing of Him who died for thee,
And hail Him as thy matchless King though all eternity.

God

Focus Verse:

A nd *God said to Moses, "I Am who I Am." And He said, "thus you shall say to the children of Israel, I Am has sent me to you. The Lord God of your fathers, the God of Abraham, the God of Isaac, and the God of Jacob, has sent me to you. This is My name forever, and this is My memorial to all generations."*

-Exodus 3:14-15

Greek: *Theos* (theh'os) the supreme Deity or Divinity.

Theological Note:

There is but one God, the Maker, Preserver and Ruler of all things, having in and of Himself, all perfections, and being infinite in them all; and to Him all creatures owe the highest love, reverence, and obedience.

-Southern Baptist Theological Seminary 1858

Pastoral Quote:

"A true love of God must begin with a delight in His holiness."

-Jonathan Edwards

Reference Verses:

The hour is coming, and now is, when the true worshippers will worship the Father in Spirit and Truth: For the Father is seeking such to worship Him. God is Spirit, and those who worship Him must worship in Spirit and Truth.

-John 4:23-24

We give You thanks, O Lord God Almighty, the One who is and was and is to come, because You have taken Your great power and reigned.

-*Revelation* 11:17

Psalm 46:1   Revelation 21:3   I John 4:19-20
John 3:16

Quote:

"It is not my ability, but my response to Gods' ability, that counts."

-Corrie Ten Boom

Commentary:

The God of the Bible is the only God. He is the living God who reigns over the universe in righteousness and holiness. This is key to understanding Christianity compared to all other world religions. All other gods are manmade, mythical, idolatrous, and demonically inspired to capture the heart of man through paganism, cults, and false religious systems. Only God is worthy of human worship for He is the loving Creator and Father. He is not the author of evil and detests all sin. He is perfect in His righteousness and can never be tempted to do evil.

There is but one God, the maker, preserver and ruler of all things, having in Himself all perfections and being infinite in them all. He is altogether "other" than us. We are made in

His image but we are not a "splinter" of Him. God is distinct from His creation and does not depend on anything or anyone. He is completely self sufficient. God cannot be fully explained by human reasoning because He is what everything else must be explained by. He is the *"all consuming fire,"* utterly opposed to anything that is opposed to Him (sin). *"The fear of the Lord is the beginning of wisdom..."* (Ps. 111:10a). God's will is certain to be accomplished and nothing in the created universe can be compared to Him.

It is vital that we understand God is not like us. He is transcendent, wholly other, morally perfect, just and holy. *"For My thoughts are not your thoughts, nor are your ways My ways"* (Isa. 55:8). We can know who God is through the revelation of Holy Scripture. The Bible reveals to us what separates God from man, what His attributes are, and we can, through His Word, grasp in part His majesty, purposes, and profound power. God has given us His Word, the Bible, so that we can know Him.

God proclaimed His name to be *"I AM"* which in the Hebrew language sounds like *"Yahweh."* Modern scholars pronounce it this way and often write it as *"Jehovah,"* which can be rendered as *"Lord."* God said to Moses that this would be His name forever (Gen. 3:15). This name signifies God's eternal nature, holiness and splendor. He is the God who rules the universe and deserves all praise and glory from His creation.

The Bible *assumes* God's existence, so there is no propulsion to *prove* He exists. Still, we can use philosophy to point people to the truth of His existence. Philosophical proofs for God's existence break down into four argumentative categories:

Teleological: the world/universe has design so there must be a Designer.

Ontological: people have an idea of a Supreme Deity (God) and could only get that idea from God Himself.

Moral: people understand right and wrong which proves there is a Moral Lawgiver. *Cosmological*: God is the First Cause of all creation.

King David, the warrior poet declared, *"The fool has said in his heart, 'there is no God"* (Psalm 14:1a).

God is Spirit (John 4:24). He was never a man who "ascended" to godhood. Through Him all other created things came into existence and it is He that sustains all. God is eternal and self-existent. This means He was never created, and will never, *not* exist. He is a personal being, not human, but He has Personhood. We are created in His image, meaning we also are spirit and have personhood.

God is Triune. He is revealed in three equally eternal Persons, the same in essence and substance but distinct in function. God the Father, God the Son, God the Holy Spirit are One. The Christian Faith is a *monotheistic* faith, meaning we worship only one God. This Trinitarian view of God is crucial for correctly defining who God is. We serve the One true God.

God is immutable (un-changing), Omnipresent (is everywhere) Omnipotent (All-powerful), Omniscient (All-knowing), Divine, and Holy. *God is love.* Our amazing God has shown His love to us through His Son and desires that all be reconciled to Him through the atoning sacrifice of Christ.

He is the Incarnate God who came down to walk among us, the One who could be touched, experiencing our weaknesses, tears, and sorrows. God knows the fragility of man, people broken by the curse of sin, and has offered the answer to our hopelessness in the Person of Jesus Christ. Jesus Christ is God, the risen Savior, who came and lived among us bringing salvation, forgiveness, truth, and eternal life. He is the true and living God, worthy of all praise and worship!

"Great is the Lord, and greatly to be praised; and His greatness is unsearchable!"

-Psalm 145:3

<u>Historical Figure:</u> *Jonathan Edwards*

Edwards was born on October 5, 1703 in Connecticut. He was a genius and entered Yale at the age of 13. He went on to be a Congregational preacher (at his grandfather's church), theologian, and missionary to Native Americans. He is widely accepted as America's most important and original philosophical theologian. He was also the leader of the "Great Awakening," a Christian Revival movement of the 1730's and 1740's most prominent in the American Colonies and Great Britain. His famous sermon, *"Sinners In the Hands of an Angry God,"* emphasized the wrath of God against sin and the dire need of God's provision of salvation in Christ. The intensity and graphic illustrations of his preaching sometimes caused people to faint. This style of preaching influenced numerous ministers of several different denominations of his time. His profound influence in American and British theology and preaching is still felt today. He died on March 22, 1758.

<u>Term:</u> *"Theophany,"* physical appearance or personal manifestation of God seen by a human being.

<u>Hymn:</u> *"Joyful, Joyful, We Adore Thee"*
  Lyrics: Henry Van Dyke (1852-1933)
  Music arranged from: Ludwig Van Beethoven (1770-1827)

Joyful, joyful, we adore Thee,
God of glory, Lord of love;
hearts unfold like flow'rs before Thee,
opening to the sun above,
melt the clouds of sin and sadness;
drive the dark of doubt away;
Giver of immortal gladness,
fill us with the light of day!

Grace

Focus verse:

*M*oreover the Law entered that the offense might
abound. But where sin abounded, grace abounded
much more, so that as sin reigned in death, even so grace
might reign through righteousness to eternal life through
Jesus Christ our Lord.

-Romans 5:20-21

Greek: *Charis* (khar'-ece) grace, benefit, favor, gift

Theological note:

The unmerited, undeserved love and acceptance of God
toward Man. Jesus Christ provides salvation for all those who
repent of their sin and receive Him as Savior and Lord. This
is not accomplished by human effort, goodness, or religious
ritual. Forgiveness of sin is a supernatural grace bestowed on
believers by faith alone in the sacrifice, and finished work of
Jesus on the cross. In experiencing divine grace there should
be a deep sense of thankfulness towards God.

Pastoral quote:

"Grace is the very opposite of merit...grace is not only undeserved favor, but it is favor shown to the one who has deserved the very opposite."

-H. A. Ironside

Reference verses:

For by grace are you saved through faith; not of yourselves; it is the gift of God, not of works lest anyone should boast.

-Ephesians 2:8-9

And He said to me, "My grace is sufficient for you, for My strength is made perfect in weakness."

-II Corinthians 12:9a

Romans 5:20   Psalm 84:11   Acts 4:33   James 4:6
II Peter 3:18

Quote:

"A man can no more take a supply of grace for the future than he can eat enough today to last him for the next six months, or take sufficient air into his lungs at once to sustain life for a week to come. We must draw upon God's boundless stores of grace from day to day as we need it."

-D.L. Moody

Commentary:

Grace is un-merited favor. Grace is getting what you do not deserve, namely, forgiveness of sin and reconciliation with God. God's grace cannot be separated from His plan of salvation. God's love and grace is what compelled Him to send His Son to die for our sin. The Gospel is full of grace and thus brings hope to sinful man.

There has been confusion about the true nature of grace. It has been twisted, as it was in Paul's day, to mean things other than its original Biblical intent. This has produced a term in our day called "cheap grace." Cheap grace adherents say that we as Christians can do anything we want without the consequences and penalty of our sin. They use grace as a license to sin. They say we are "under grace" and the Law of God is no longer in effect and we do not have an obligation to obey it. This is known as "antinomianism" (*against the law)* and has caused much confusion, pain and spiritual bondage within the Body of Christ.

Obeying the Law of God cannot save us, only faith in Christ can accomplish salvation. But through grace we are now free to practice righteousness, free to obey God's Word, and in turn, to do good works because of our love for Him. We should never live in a way that takes for granted the grace of God. We should never trivialize the sacrifice of Christ that has placed us in a position of being righteous and justified.

Grace is not cheap, sin is not harmless, and the Law is fulfilled in Christ. The grace of God is seen most clearly when we look to the cross of Jesus. God's sinless Son hanging suspended between Heaven and earth, bearing our sin and shame, taking our penalty and our certain future of Hell upon Himself. We did not deserve in any way this amazing outpouring of love and deliverance. ***"For by grace you have been saved..."*** (Eph. 2:8a). Grace is a gift to us from God and that gift cost Him everything of worth.

Any view of grace that leaves out the atonement of Christ is false. Without Calvary we could never be forgiven by God and therefore we would be condemned and hopeless. It is the astounding price of Jesus' blood that takes away our sin. We should daily praise and serve the One who so tremendously held out His love to those so utterly lost and helpless. As we experience divine grace there should be a deep sense of thankfulness towards the Lord. What a gift. What a Savior!

"In Him we have redemption through His blood, the forgiveness of sins, according to the riches of His grace, which He made to abound toward us in all wisdom and prudence."

-Ephesians 1:7-8

Historical Figure: *A.W. Tozer*

Aidan Wilson Tozer was born April 21, 1897 in western Pennsylvania. He was a Protestant pastor, preacher, author, Bible conference speaker, and spiritual mentor. He accepted an offer to pastor a church before he got his ministry license. That pastorate led to 44 years of powerful evangelical ministry. His book, *The Pursuit Of God,* has been an important work calling the Church back to holiness. He died on May 12, 1963.

Term: *"Sola Gratia,"* Latin for *"Grace alone."* Reformed theological teaching that states God redeems and pardons man without any merit of our own, but based solely on the grace and sacrifice of Christ alone.

Hymn: *"Grace Greater Than All Our Sin"*
    Words: Julia H. Johnston, 1910
    Music: Daniel B. Towner, 1910

Marvelous grace of our loving Lord,
grace that exceeds our sin and our guilt, yonder on
Calvary's mount outpoured,
There where the blood of the Lamb was spilt.
Grace, grace, God's grace, grace that will pardon
and cleanse with-in;
Grace, grace, God's grace,
grace that is greater than all our sin.

Heaven

Focus verse:

L *et not your heart be troubled; you believe in God, believe also in Me. In My Father's house are many mansions; if it were not so I would have told you. I go to prepare a place for you. And if I go to prepare a place for you, I will come again and receive you to Myself, that where I am, there you may be also.*

-John 14:1-3

Greek: *Ouranos* (oo-ran-os') Heaven, the dwelling place of God

Theological note:
    Heaven, the dwelling place of God, is above the earth and space. God created Heaven and the angelic realm and all are under His Lordship. Jesus Christ is seated in Heaven at the right hand of God the Father (Ephesians 1:20). Heaven is the eternal home of all believers.

Pastoral quote:

"We talk about Heaven being so far away. It is within speaking distance to those who belong there. Heaven is a prepared place for a prepared people."

-D.L. Moody
American pastor, evangelist
(1837-1899)

Reference verses:

Do not lay up for yourselves treasures on earth, where moth and rust destroy and where thieves break in and steal; But lay up for yourselves treasure in Heaven, where neither moth or rust destroys and where thieves do not break in and steal.

-Matthew 6:19-20

They raised their voice to God with one accord and said, "Lord, You are God, who made Heaven and earth and the sea and all that is in them."

-Acts 4:24

Ephesians 1:20   Matt. 11:25   II Corinthians 5:1-2
II Corinthians 12:2-4   Luke 10:20

Quote:

"The way the world responds to the world's decay is to engage equally in idiot hopes and idiot despairs. On the one hand some new discovery or policy is expected to put everything right. A new fuel, a new drug, a world government...or some disaster confidently will prove to be our undoing: Capitalism will break down, fuel will run out, atomic bombs will lay us low, atomic waste will kill us off.

Overpopulation will suffocate us or a declining birthrate will put us at the mercy of our enemies.

In Christian terms such hopes and fears are equally beside the point. For as Christians we know here we have no continuing city, crowns roll in the dust, because every earthly kingdom at some point will fall and be no more. But we acknowledge a King that man did not crown and men cannot dethrone. As we are citizens of the City of God that man did not build, and cannot destroy."

-Malcolm Muggeridge
British Journalist and Author
(1903-1990)

Commentary:

Heaven is the dwelling place of God. Jesus is seated at the right hand of the throne of the Father. For deceased Christians and all Old Testament era believers, Heaven is where they live at this very moment. The Bible teaches that at death humans are immediately ushered into the presence of God if they have placed their trust in Jesus. Those who have rejected Christ will lift up their eyes in Hell when they die.

Heaven is a real place occupied by redeemed people who have passed on and the angelic host. It is far from the strange concepts that permeate society such as chubby angelic babies sitting on clouds playing harps, or a paradise where you do whatever you want to do with whomever, or whatever you desire. Heaven is not about our personal pleasure nor is it Nirvana where we all just blend back into the universe. Heaven is Heaven because God is there and we are in His glorious presence.

Heaven is the divine headquarters where God rules over the universe. We as Christians are to rejoice that our names are written in Heaven (Luke 10:20). God has promised us an eternal home immersed in celebration, joy, happiness, and blessing. Paul said, *"Eye has not seen, nor ear heard, nor have entered into the heart of man the things which God has prepared for those who love Him"* (I Cor. 2:9). We need to understand that the things we do *not* see are as real, and actually more lasting, than what we do see in our temporal life on earth (II Cor. 4:16-18).

The Word declares that the hope of Heaven is the hope of glory. Those who have this hope are all who are saved by faith in Jesus Christ. Also babies who have died (including miscarriages, stillborn, and those aborted), people born with severe mental impairment, and children who have died before reaching the age of accountability (*ability to understand the concept and reality of their sin*), are covered by God's mercy and grace and will enter Heaven. In a world stained by death, you can take comfort in knowing that you will see your deceased child and Christian loved ones again in Heaven. What a tremendous reality to know that we as believers are not home yet. This earthly life is not all there is and what is coming is beyond human comprehension.

In Heaven there is no sickness, death, tears, hatred, prejudice, darkness, sorrow, or sin. We will be free forever from the curse of sin, death and wickedness. We will rule and reign with Christ. There will be no marriage in Heaven (Luke 20:34-36) because we will be in perfect relationships with all who dwell there. We, as the Bride of Christ, will desire and love Jesus above any former earthly relationship, and we will be of one mind, one purpose, completely in unity. We will serve Him forever in our resurrected bodies and we will have perfect fellowship with God. The Bible says that every nation and people group will be represented in Heaven. All those throughout history who have called upon the name of Jesus from every part of the world will be in Heaven eternally.

According to the Word when we are saved we immediately become a citizen of Heaven (Phil. 3:20). Of course this does not mean we are there yet but we do have citizenship. When we visit another country we have a passport that declares we are citizens of the United States of America. We are no longer physically in the USA but we still have the rights and benefits of citizenship. This is why many Christians through the centuries have compared our earthly life to a journey, and that we are only passing through a "foreign" land as we travel towards our real home.

The Bible says that Heaven and earth will pass away and God will create a new Heaven and earth sometime in the future. This re-creation will be permanent. (Isaiah 65:17, 66:22) The New Jerusalem will be a part of this re-creation and we will dwell with Christ there for eternity. This Heavenly City will descend from Heaven and will be brilliantly beautiful in form and function. In this City will be found the Tree of Life, the River of Life, and joyous communion with God and His people (Rev. ch. 20-22).

God will declare at this time in history, *"Behold I make all things new!"* God also states emphatically, *"...these words are faithful and true,"* and *"It is done!"* Heaven is a certainty for those who have placed their trust in Christ. Even though we lose our loved ones to death in this earthly life, we can be assured that if they are in Christ, they will be very much a part of our future.

To be a part of this present (and coming) reality and the hope of Heaven our names must be written in the *Lamb's Book of Life* (Rev. 20:12). How can you know your name will be found in the Book? Receive Jesus Christ as your Lord and Savior, call on Him to save you from your sin, believing that He is the risen Lord and He will create in you a new heart and a new eternal destination.

Our Father in Heaven, hallowed be Your name. Your Kingdom come, Your will be done on earth as it is in Heaven.

-Matthew 6: 9-10

Historical Figure: *D.L. Moody*

Dwight Lyman Moody was born February 5, 1837 in Northfield, Massachusetts. He was one of the greatest American evangelists winning over one million souls to Jesus Christ during his ministry. Moody was led to Christ as a teenager by his Sunday School teacher Edward Kimball while visiting the shoe store where Moody worked.

D.L. did not have any formal ministry or school training beyond the typical elementary education of the day. God called him to preach shortly after he was saved and he went on to pastor a church that eventually became the Moody Church. His ministry also produced the Moody schools in Massachusetts, as well as the Moody Bible Institute and Moody Publishers. He was a prominent figure in the American and British revivals of the late 1800's. When in England he would preach at C.H. Spurgeon's church.

Moody was the first to do widespread "evangelistic campaigns" using Ira Sankey as his featured singer and worship leader. They would sometimes hold meetings that would draw 10,000 to 20,000 people at a time. He promoted ministry to Civil War soldiers, religious training for women, the YMCA, development of "Sunday Schools," and training young people for domestic and international missions. Moody's influence on modern evangelism and ministry methods are deep and far reaching.

Term: *"Pantheism,"* the belief that God and the universe are the same. Denying the personality of God and seeing God and nature as intertwined and that God is within everything. This is a belief found in pagan religious systems like Wicca and Hinduism.

<u>Hymn:</u> *"When We All Get To Heaven"*
     Lyrics: Eliza E. Hewitt, 1898
     Music: "Heaven," Emily D. Wilson, 1898

Sing the wondrous love of Jesus, Sing His mercy and His grace: in the mansions bright and blessed, He'll prepare for us a place.
When we all get to Heaven, what a day of rejoicing that will be, when we all see Jesus, we'll sing and shout the victory!

Hell

Focus verse:

*A**nd if your eye causes you to sin, pluck it out and cast it from you. It is better for you to enter into life with one eye, rather than having two eyes, to be cast into hell fire.*

-Matthew 18:9

Greek: *Geenna* (gheh-en-nah) Valley of Hinnom, a name for the place of eternal punishment.
Hades (hah-dace) place of the damned, grave, hell

Theological note:

Hell is the abode of the wicked dead, specifically a place of torment and separation from God. The location of eternal punishment for all who have rejected the grace and salvation of God through Jesus Christ.

Pastoral Quote:

"When preaching on Hell, one should have tears in their eyes."

-D.L. Moody

Reference verses:

The rich man also died and was buried. And being in torments in Hell, he lifted up his eyes and saw Abraham afar off, and Lazarus in his bosom. Then he cried and said, "Father Abraham, have mercy on me and send Lazarus that he may dip the tip of his finger in water and cool my tongue; for I am tormented in these flames."

-Luke 16:22-24

And death and Hell were cast into the Lake of Fire. This is the second death. And whosoever was not found written in the Book of Life was cast into the Lake of Fire.

-Revelation 20:14-15

Revelation 20:10   Psalm 16:9-10   Isaiah 5:14
Matthew 13: 41-42

Quote:

"As the Lord liveth, sinner, thou standest on a single plank over the mouth of Hell, and that plank is rotten."
-Charles Haddon Spurgeon
British Baptist minister,
theologian, author (1834-1892)

Commentary:

The first statement in the New Testament about Hell came from the lips of Jesus in Matthew chapter 5. Jesus says clearly that Hell is a place of punishment and fire. Many teachers and ministers today try to "spiritualize" Hell. They say that Hell is not a real place but it just symbolizes the separation of men from God. Another common false teaching is the *"annihilation of the wicked dead"* which says that lost people will burn for a period of time and then vanish forever as if they never existed. The Catholic doctrine of *Purgatory* is also not taught in the Bible. It is important as believers in Christ to have a clear Biblical understanding of Hell. Why? Because so much is at stake.

Jesus taught that Hell is a place of damnation (Matt. 23:33). He is the first to use the term *"hell fire"* and He used it many times. Jesus was the original "hell-fire" preacher (Mark 9:43-48). He taught that Hell was eternal, and that it was created after the heavenly rebellion for the Devil and his angels. Hell was not originally intended for man (Matt. 25:41). Jesus spoke more about Hell than He did about Heaven. We need to heed His Word.

Jesus tells the story of the Rich man and Lazarus in Luke 16. This is not a parable but a true account of a past event. This story gives us a glimpse into Hell. From this account we understand that Hell is a holding place for the unsaved dead and a place of fire. We understand that in Hell a person has a body, they can see, feel, speak, desire, remember, cry, beg, and thirst. It is clear that when a lost person dies they will immediately open their eyes in this place of torment.

From Scripture we derive that Hell is located in the depths of the earth. In Ephesians 4:8-10, Numbers 16:28-33, Acts 2:25-28, and Jesus Himself said in Matthew 12:38-40 that He would descend into the *lower parts of the earth*. Keep in mind that Jesus did not descend into Hell's fire during His three days in the grave. The idea that Jesus had to burn in Hell for our sin is an absolute heresy. Jesus suffered on the cross, not in Hell.

Before Christ's resurrection and since the beginning of the Fall, *Hades* consisted of *two* compartments. On one side was *Paradise* and across the great chasm was *Hell*. Old Testament believers at death, from Adam to the time of Christ, went immediately to *Paradise*. They could not enter Heaven because Jesus the Messiah had not yet shed His blood on Calvary and physically atoned for their sin.

Jesus said to the thief on the cross, *"Today you shall be with Me in Paradise"* (Luke 23:39-43) because Jesus (during His 3 days in the tomb) would appear in Hades and declare to all those held there, including those in Hell, that He was indeed the Messiah, the Son of God. Those believers in Paradise from Adam, Noah, Abraham, David, the thief, and all others now had the right to righteously enter into Heaven where today they abide.

Isaiah 5:14 states that Hell would be enlarged. Now that the Paradise dwelling of Hades is no longer needed it is used entirely as a holding place for the dead who have rejected Christ in this life. Eventually Hell will be cast into the *Lake of Fire* (Rev. 20:14).

Hell is a reality that we as Christians must take seriously. If we discount it or say it does not exist we are calling Jesus a liar. We should care enough about our fellow man to tell them the Good News that Jesus has destroyed the curse of everlasting death and holds out salvation as a free gift to all who will come to Him. We must also realize that no one has an excuse to walk away from the grace of God (Romans 1:18-2:1).

Jesus Christ is not some angry God who delights in throwing people into Hell. Actually, He is blocking the very gateway to Hell with His own life. The life He willingly gave for us upon the cross. Jesus today is standing with His arms open wide with nail-scarred hands, beckoning all to come and be saved. He is pleading for man to come to Heaven through the only Door that leads away from certain destruction. He *is* the door that leads to eternal life and joy. People who find themselves in Hell are those who literally had to stumble over Jesus Christ and His free gift of salvation... stubbornly choosing for themselves to go there for eternity.

God reveals His truth, salvation and His glory to all that honestly seek Him in all nations and people groups. Even the heavens and all creation declare the glory of God (Psalm

19:1). The problem is that many people will choose to reject God's truth and believe a lie, walking in rebellion, selfishness, greed, lust, false religion, and wickedness. They willfully have turned from the revelation of God, and God must allow them, as freewill agents, to choose eternal death.

Rarely do people actually reject Christ on an intellectual level. The reality is that they do not want to submit their lives to God, desiring to fulfill the lust of their flesh and proceed to justify their rebellion and pride with worldly philosophies and arguments. *God is just and He is fair.* He will not force anyone who will not worship Him in this life to worship Him in the next.

May we urgently and intently hold forth the Word of Life in our generation to everyone we encounter with the hope and amazing grace of God who desires that *all* people are saved (II Peter 3:9). The Church is commissioned to proclaim the *Gospel*, the shining hope that faith in Christ conquers Hell and the grave. That *is* Good News!

"I am the door. If anyone enters by Me, he will be saved."

-John 10:9a

Historical Figure: *Hudson Taylor*

Taylor (1832-1905) was a British Protestant Christian missionary to China, and founder of the China Inland Mission. He spent 51 years of his life in China. The society he began produced over 800 missionaries, 205 mission stations, 125 schools, and resulted in over 125,000 Christian conversions. At the age of 19 he said he realized *"that a man could take God at His Word,"* and that was the moment Hudson decided to trust Christ with every area of his life. His love for the people of China and his passion for evangelism literally changed a nation. Taylor's influence on the modern mission movement is still felt today.

Term: *"Atheism," "a"* meaning *no, "theo"* meaning *God.* The belief that there is no God.

Hymn: *"There Is A Fountain"*
    Words: William Cowper, 1771
    Music: *Cleansing Fountain*, Early American Melody.

There is a fountain filled with blood,
flows through Immanuel's veins;
and sinners plunged beneath that flood,
lose all their guilty stains:
lose all their guilty stains,
lose all their guilty stains;
and sinners plunged beneath that flood,
lose all their guilty stains.

The Holy Bible

Focus verse:

*K*nowing this first, that no prophecy of Scripture is of private interpretation, for prophecy never came by the will of man, but holy men of God spoke as they were moved by the Holy Spirit.

-II Peter 1:20-21

Greek: *Graphe* (graf-ay') a document, scripture

Theological Note:

The reformers of the 16th Century understood the unique authority of the Bible using the Latin phrase, "Sola Scriptura" meaning, "the Scripture alone." They upheld Scripture as *"the only infallible rule of faith and practice."* Orthodox, historical Christianity has always contended that the Old Testament and New Testament Scriptures are inspired by God through the Holy Spirit and are absolute truth. These writings of the Old Testament Prophets and New Testament Apostles are the authoritative rule of all saving knowledge, faith, and obedience.

Pastoral Quote:

"There's a big difference between the books that men make and the Book that makes men."

–Unknown

"The Bible will keep you from sin, or sin will keep you from the Bible."

-D.L. Moody

Reference Verses:

Jesus answered him, saying, "It is written, man shall not live by bread alone, but by every word of God."

-Luke 4:4

We do not follow cleverly invented stories when we told you about the power and coming of the Lord Jesus Christ, but we were eyewitnesses to His majesty.

-II Peter 1:16

Isaiah 55:8-9   Psalm 119:105   John 1:14
Isaiah 55:11   I Peter 1:25

Quote:

"I have read in Plato and Cicero sayings that are wise and very beautiful; But I have never read in either of them; 'Come unto Me all ye that labor and are heavy laden and I will give you rest."

-Saint Augustine of Hippo
Latin philosopher, theologian
(354-430)

Commentary:

The main focus of the Bible is the redeeming work of Jesus Christ reconciling sinful man to a Holy God. Jesus is the *Word*, the *Logos*. He is all the Truth that can be known (John 1:14). He is creator God, Savior, and Redeemer. The Bible is God's divine revelation of His purposes in Jesus, the Son. II Timothy 3:15-17 states, *"And that from a child thou hast known the Holy Scriptures, which are able to make thee wise unto salvation through faith which is in Christ Jesus. All Scripture is given by inspiration of God, and is profitable for reproof, for correction, for instruction in righteousness."*

The Christian Bible is composed of 66 books written by 40 authors inspired by the Holy Spirit, from 3 continents and 3 languages, (Hebrew, Aramaic, and Greek), over a span of approximately 1500 years. The assurance that Scripture is from God to His people is attested to by Jesus Christ and His apostles. The Bible's contents from Genesis through Revelation should be revered as God's authoritative instructions to all Believers.

Manuscript evidence: The Bible is the most documented ancient writing in history. There are 5,750 Greek texts, 8000 Latin texts, and 11,000 other various texts, in all over 25,000 to study and observe, with some copies only 120 years from their original texts. Within 300 years of Jesus' ascension we had our first complete New Testament.

"Higher critics" (those who attack the veracity of the Bible's authors) claim the Bible should be thrown out for "text uncertainty" because the manuscript evidence is too far removed from the original writings. *If that is the case we would have to throw out all ancient writings.* No exceptions. Why? Here are some popular examples: Caesar's *"Gaelic Wars,"* most current copy for study was written 1,000 years after his death. All Plato's writings: most current copies are 1,300 years after his death. Homer's *"The Odyssey,"* most current copies are 2,200 years after his death. For all these writings mentioned there are less than *10 each* in existence to study and observe.

The New Testament has been sealed by the blood of Christ for all eternity. Unshakeable truth, unchanging, eternal. We see throughout history the immense attack by Satan to destroy the Word. His most basic assault is to always cast doubt upon the Word of God. He did it in the Garden of Eden and he still does it today. As Christians we must always be willing to stand for the integrity and faithful transliteration of the Bible.

We do not worship the Bible; we worship the God of the Bible who gave us His Word in written form through human agents inspired by the Holy Spirit. The Christian Faith is founded on these authoritative writings of the New Testament Apostles and the Old Testament Prophets. May we be diligent in maintaining scriptural integrity by always comparing modern translations with the earliest ancient Hebrew and Greek manuscripts that are copies of the original inerrant and infallible Scriptures ("scripture" means "writing").*"Forever, O Lord, Your Word is settled in Heaven"* (Ps. 119:89).

Critics also attack the veracity of the Bible by comparing it to other major religion's sacred texts, deeming them all to be fallible or worthy as any of the others. The problem with this criticism is that all these other "sacred" writings of the world religions were written by men who said they were visited by an angel, spirits, gods, etc. Their religious system was built on what they say they were told by these entities to reveal to the world, with no witnesses to the "divine" encounter, and then these men died.

The Bible was written by men who encountered the living God. Christianity is built upon Holy Scripture inspired by the Holy Spirit who spoke through the Apostles and the Prophets. The main difference between the Christian Bible and all other religious writings is that the New Testament Apostles <u>saw</u> the Risen Lord. Many of them died a martyr's death because they would not deny the resurrection of Jesus Christ or His teaching. They could not *un-see* the Truth even if it cost them their lives. There were many other witnesses to what they declared as the truth. These same apostles, and certainly Jesus Himself, also attested to the veracity of the Old Testament scriptures that ultimately pointed to the coming Messiah, Jesus Christ, and His Kingdom.

The Bible is approximately 30% prophetic and entirely accurate. This in itself distinguishes the Word of God from all other books. All other major religious "prophets" never had even *one* of their "prophecies" fulfilled. Only the Holy Bible establishes this massive prophetic evidence throughout history on such a scale that to deny it as divine revelation is absurd.

Not only is the Bible prophetically accurate it is historically accurate. Archeologists have used its detailed information to help guide them in finding ancient cities and kingdoms. Dr. Nelson Glueck, an Israeli modern expert in archeology stated, *"Scores of archeological findings have been made which confirm in clear outline or in exact detail historical statements in the Bible. And by the same token, proper evaluation of Biblical descriptions has often led to amazing discoveries."*

The Bible is also scientifically accurate. The Bible records principles of modern science long before they were discovered by modern era scientists. Some of those mentioned in Scripture are: the Earth is a sphere (Isaiah 40:22), the hydrologic cycle (Ecclesiastes 1:7), the vital importance of blood in life processes (Leviticus 17:11), gravitational field (Job 26:7), vastness of the universe (Isaiah 55:9), law of conservation of mass and energy (II Peter 3:7), the Earth is suspended in space (Job 26:7), and many others. The Bible is reliable and true in all aspects of life.

The *Canon* (the *"rule"*) of Scripture is seen as the *"Vox Dei,"* the *"voice of God"* on earth. We are to submit our thoughts, actions, and standards to the Bible. How do we do this? We must be in the Word often. Be diligent to study the Bible on your own, in a small group, and in church. *Always study the Bible in context*, not just a verse here or there. Taking a verse or passage out of context without understanding the surrounding Scripture verses can lead to confusion, wrong conclusions, and eventually heretical teaching and thinking. This is why it is so important to attend a Christ centered, Bible believing, and teaching church.

The Word of God releases the Holy Spirit to do His work bringing down strongholds, upholding truth, and initiating salvation. *God's Holy Spirit never works contrary to His Word.* The Word is living and powerful and our obedience to Christ brings wisdom and life. The Word will change your life, for it is the primary transforming agent on the planet. The Word of God, through the power of the Holy Spirit, can change the human heart.

Be a student of the Bible and study the Word with the knowledge that *Scripture interprets Scripture*. We must be aware that spiritual understanding of the Bible (*illumination*) is imparted by the Holy Spirit (I Cor. 2:10-16). This is why those who are not saved, not being indwelled by the Holy Spirit, cannot fully understand the Bible, and even regard it as "foolishness." To those who attack the Bible with the standard line, *"Prove to me the Bible is true,"* I believe it is fair to reply, *"Prove to me it is not."*

God's Word is the standard we are to live by. We are to **"...be doers of the Word, not hearers only..."** (James 1:22). We should never compare ourselves to each other to see if we are "measuring up" in regards to our faith. God's Truth cuts deep and is the only measuring method that will clearly define an uncompromised life. Are you seeking wisdom and truth? Go to the source. Build your life on the solid foundation of the Word.

"For the Word of God is living and powerful, and sharper than any two-edged sword, piercing even to the division of soul and spirit, and joints and marrow, and is a discerner of the thoughts and intents of the heart."

-Hebrews 4:12

Historical Figure: *William Tyndale*

William Tyndale, born in 1494, is known as the *"Captain of the Army of Reformers."* Tyndale was a true scholar and a genius, fluent in 8 languages. He is also known as the *"Architect of the English language."* When the Catholic Church found out about his plans to translate the Bible into English they constantly sent inquisitors and bounty hunters after him to stop it. Tyndale's New Testament was the first to come directly from the Greek text and was produced in 1525. The Catholic Church burned every copy they could find. They knew that if people read the Word for themselves they would soon realize that the Pope's supreme authority, salvation by works, selling of indulgences, purgatory, canonizing Saints, Mary's co-redemptive position, and the need for Priests would be seen as unbiblical and they would lose their authority over the people and the enormous amount of money they brought in by these false doctrines. In 1535, Tyndale was arrested, and jailed for over a year, tried for heresy and burned at the stake in 1536 by Catholic Church Officials. Tyndale's personal mission was to translate the Word of God, the Holy Bible, into the English of his day and breaking it free from Catholic oppression. His passion was that all people, poor, rich, weak, or strong could hold the Bible in their hands and read it for themselves. He is one of the most important figures of the Reformation Period. The

King James 1611 Bible translators used most of Tyndale's earlier translation to complete theirs.

Term: *"Transliterate,"* to change words or letters into a corresponding alphabet or language. Example: the Greek *"x"* is *"ch"* in English.

Hymn: *"O Word of God Incarnate"*
       Lyrics: William W. How, 1867
       Music: *Munich*, adapted by Felix Mendelssohn,
       1847

O Word of God Incarnate,
O Wisdom from on high,
O Truth unchanged, unchanging,
O Light of our dark sky,
We praise Thee for the radiance
that from the hallowed page,
a lantern to our footsteps,
shines on from age to age.

Holy Spirit

Focus Verse:

*H*owever, when He, the Spirit of Truth, has come, He will guide you into all truth; for He will not speak on His own authority, but whatever He hears He will speak; and He will tell you things to come.

-John 16:13

Greek: *Pneuma* (pnyoo'mah) breath, Christ's Spirit, divine

Theological Note:

The Holy Spirit is the third Person of the Trinity. The apostle John called Him the *Paracletos*, or translated, the *Helper*. The work of the Helper, the Spirit of God, is carried out by a Personal Being. He can speak (Acts 1:16), Witness (John 15:26), Will (I Cor. 12:11), Teach (John 14:26) and Intercede (Romans 8:26-27). All of these are acts of an individual Person. The Holy Spirit is God, eternally One with the Father and Son.

Pastoral Quote:

"Do not pray for more of the Holy Spirit. The Holy Spirit is the third Person of the Trinity and is not in pieces.

Every child of God has all of Him, but does He have all of us?"

-F.B. Meyer

Reference Verses:

If you then, being evil, know how to give good gifts to your children, how much more will your Heavenly Father give the Holy Spirit to those who ask Him!

-Luke 11:13

For you did not receive the spirit of bondage again to fear, but you received the spirit of adoption by whom we cry out, "Abba, Father." The Spirit Himself bears witness with our spirit that we are the children of God.

-Romans 8:15-16

Galatians 3:14   John 14:16-17   Acts 5: 1-4
Isaiah 59:21   John 7:38-39

Quote:

"Sadly enough, there is a kind of anti-intellectualism among many Christians: spirituality is falsely pitted against intellectual comprehension as though they stood in a dichotomy. Such anti-intellectualism cuts away at the very heart of the Christian message. Of course there is a false intellectualism which does destroy the work of the Holy Spirit. But it does not arise when men wrestle honestly with honest questions and then see that the Bible has the answers. This does not oppose true spirituality."

-Francis Schaeffer

Commentary:

The Holy Spirit is God. He is the third Person of the Trinity. In John chapter 14 Jesus says to His disciples that God will give them another "Helper" which will be the Spirit of Truth. This word *helper* is translated from the Greek word *paracletos*. A *paraclete* was an advocate in a legal sense, a lawyer. It also means one who helps, counsels, brings strength and provides encouragement. The Holy Spirit was given to carry out the teaching and the testimony of Jesus Christ through the Body of Christ, the Church.

All Apostolic writers of the New Testament witnessed to the power and function of the Holy Spirit. The book of Acts (*acts* of the Apostles) has also been called the "Acts of the Holy Spirit" because of the focus on the work of the Holy Spirit (Holy Ghost) throughout Luke's account of the early Church. The Apostle Paul's writings give us further theological framing of the Holy Spirit's work within the life of the believer and the mission of the Church. The Holy Spirit is a Personal Being equal to the Father and the Son, worthy of worship, glory, honor, love and obedience. The main work of the Holy Spirit is to glorify Jesus Christ.

Another proof that the Holy Spirit is God is that only God deserves a temple. At conversion we become the temple of God as the Holy Spirit takes up residence in the life of the Christian believer at the exact moment of regeneration (I Cor. 3:16). When we are saved by placing our faith in Jesus, the Spirit of God indwells us, making us a new creation, bestowing spiritual gifts, bringing illumination (understanding the Bible), and guiding us through the sanctification process. It is by the power of the Holy Spirit that we are baptized into the fellowship and life of the resurrected Christ Jesus.

The only sin that God will not forgive, the *unpardonable sin* (Matt. 12:31-32), is blasphemy against the Holy Spirit. *This is not a sin a Christian can commit.* It is the sin of unregenerate people attributing the work of God to the work of Satan. It is when man sees a true work of God and says that it is evil and has no worth.

The work of the Holy Spirit is to lead people to Jesus Christ for salvation (John 16:8). When a person deliberately shuns the light of Christ and the conviction of their sins by His Spirit, they are willfully setting their hearts and minds against the *will* of the Son of God, calling redemption useless and evil. There is nothing more serious to God than the shedding of Jesus' blood on the cross. This ongoing rejection of Christ's sacrificial gift begins to harden one's heart resulting in a final rejection of Jesus as Redeemer. At this point the Holy Spirit will no longer convict that person of their need for the Savior and God will give them over to a reprobate heart. Only God knows that moment when a person crosses this tragic line, forsaking salvation, and now forever lost in their sin. This is why the invitation to trust Jesus as Lord and Savior is always *today,* not later (Heb. 3:7-15).

The Holy Spirit is a member of the Godhead and they are One. This truth is revealed throughout the Bible and within the context of the mystery of the Trinity. The Holy Spirit brings conviction to the lost man and faith to those who seek the Lord for salvation. He is the One who brings strength to our lives, ever interceding in prayer for us, and gives the *"peace that passes all understanding."* How awesome that Almighty God truly lives within those who are called by His Name. We are the temple of God and He is closer than a friend.

"Or do you not know that your body is the temple of the Holy Spirit who is in you, whom you have from God, and you are not your own? For you were bought at a price; therefore glorify God in your body and in your spirit, which are God's."

-I Corinthians 6:19-20

<u>Historical Figure</u>: *Donald Cargill*

Donald Cargill was a Scottish Presbyterian minister who opposed the Anglican Church in Scotland in the mid to late 1600's. He and other Presbyterian pastors were known as "Covenanters" and they refused to acknowledge the King of England, Charles II, as the head of the Church. Cargill stated that only Jesus Christ is the Head of the Church. This brought much persecution to these men of God. Many of these pastors were hunted down, tortured, and then killed. Cargill was banned from Scotland but would secretly go into Scottish towns and villages and preach the Gospel until the royal soldiers would find out. He would then hide and slip into another town to preach. He was wounded and left for dead several times in his encounters with English forces but God spared his life and he continued to preach. In 1681 he and several other Covenanters were captured by the English and a few days later were tried and found guilty for teaching that Jesus Christ was the Head of the Church. They were beheaded publicly on July 27, 1681. As Cargill climbed the steps to the executioner's block he said, *"The Lord knows I go up this ladder with less fear and anxiety than I entered the pulpit to preach."* In 1688 William III became king and re-established the Presbyterian Church in Scotland.

<u>Term:</u> *"Saints,"* Holy people, all those who belong to God and are indwelled by His Holy Spirit. The Church. Sometimes erroneously used to designate a small group of dedicated believers or people who have achieved "sainthood."

<u>Hymn:</u> *"Spirit of the Living God"*
Words and Music: Daniel Iverson, 1926

Spirit of the Living God,
fall fresh on me;
Spirit of the Living God,

fall fresh on me.
Break me, melt me,
mold me, fill me.
Spirit of the Living God,
fall fresh on me.

Jesus Christ the Mediator

Focus Verse:

*H**e (God) has delivered us from the power of darkness and conveyed us into the Kingdom of the Son of His love, in whom we have redemption through His blood, the forgiveness of sins.*

-Colossians 1:13-14

Greek: *Mesites (mes-ee'-tace)* a go between, one who mediates between two parties.

Theological Note:

Jesus Christ, the only begotten Son of God is the divinely appointed Mediator between God and man. Having taken upon himself human nature yet without sin, He perfectly fulfilled the law, suffered and died upon the Cross for the Salvation of sinful man. He became the Mediator of the New Covenant, establishing it through His death and blood, ever interceding for His people.

Pastoral Quote:

"By Christ's purchasing redemption, two things are intended, His sanctification and His merit. All is done by

the price that Christ lays down, which does two things: it pays our debt and so it satisfies; By it's intrinsic value and by agreement between Father and Son it procures our tithe and so it merits. The satisfaction of Christ is to free us from misery and the merit of Christ is to purchase happiness for us."

-Jonathan Edwards
American Clergyman,
Theologian (1703-1757)

Reference Verses:

To Jesus the Mediator of the new covenant, and to the blood of sprinkling that speaks better things than that of Abel.

-Hebrews 12:24

For there is one God, and one Mediator between God and men. The man, Christ Jesus, who gave himself a ransom for all, to be testified in due time.

-I Timothy 2:5-6

Hebrews 8:16   Hebrews 9:15   Galatians 3:19-20

Quote:

"We believe that Salvation of sinners is wholly Grace; through the Mediatorial offices of the Son of God; who by appointment of the Father took upon Him our nature, yet without sin: honored the Divine Law by His personal obedience, and by His death made a full atonement for sins."
- Baptist Church Manual

Commentary:

We cannot establish our righteousness before God because we have all sinned. We need a Mediator, an advocate who stands with us in the presence of the holiness of God Almighty. Leviticus 17:11 states clearly that *"...it is the blood that makes atonement for your soul."* Atonement means to bring two alienated parties back together. This is done by a mediator who is a "go between." As sinners we have no merit or standing on our own before God and we must have a mediator to insure our salvation. This atonement for our sin can only be fulfilled by God's Son who stands between us and God the Father claiming us as His own. In return, God declares us forgiven and righteous because we are washed in the blood of Christ and made a new creation.

In a world drowning in sin and depravity, Scripture reveals God's grace towards man. Where we are hopelessly inadequate to amend for our sins, God supplies the atonement our sin made necessary, and He demands. Christ's precious blood shed for the redemption of man is the crimson thread of atonement that runs throughout the Word of God, from Genesis to Revelation, offering hope to the hopeless.

The Old Testament animal sacrificial system was a "type" and "shadow" that pointed to something better and lasting: The *Anti-type,* Jesus, the sinless Lamb of God. On Calvary Jesus' blood poured from His wounds, drenching His cross, and forever displaying to the world the gruesome reality that forgiveness of sin exacts a brutal and tremendous price. During that very specific moment in history all creation groaned as Jesus paid the ultimate price for our sin with His precious life. A price you and I could never pay. In that one sacrificial act Jesus demonstrated that He is the only way for man to be reconciled to God.

Jesus is the Son of God. He is the only way to the Father (John 14:6) because He alone is worthy to stand before a Holy God and secure our redemption. It was Jesus who took our punishment for our sin and has paid the ransom for our deliverance. Only the Son of God could bear this crushing debt. He is the Lamb slain before the foundation of the world, and He alone can stand before the Father and present us free and clean.

If you are wrong about Jesus, you will be wrong about everything else that truly matters. All Jesus has for you is Life. Trust Christ to be your Savior and Advocate.

The next day John saw Jesus coming toward him, and said, "Behold! The Lamb of God who takes away the sin of the world!"

-John 1:29

Historical Figure: *David Brainerd*

David Brainerd was born in Haddam, Connecticut on April 20, 1718. He was a missionary to the American Indians and is one of the most influential missionaries of all time. Even though he died at an early age, his impact on missionaries has been profound. During his life he suffered many hardships and wrote a journal and diary throughout his life that was published by Jonathan Edwards, who was greatly impacted by David's short ministry. Brainerd pursued an education at Yale, but was denied a degree and reevaluated the direction of his life. He became an ordained Presbyterian minister in 1744, and began his powerful three year ministry to the American Indians. When tuberculosis weakened him he moved into Jonathan Edwards home for his final months of life under the care of Edwards' daughter, Jerusha. He died 19 weeks later on October 9, 1747 as what he referred to in his diary, *"that glorious day."*

Term: *"Hermeneutics,"* The art of finding an authors meaning and explaining it to others. The art of preaching.

<u>**Hymn**</u>: *"O Sacred Head, Now Wounded"*
Words: Paul Gerhardt, 1656 Medieval Latin Poem.
Translated 1830 by James W. Alexander.
Music: Passion Chorale, Hans Leo Hassler 1601
Harmonized By: J.S. Bach 1729

O Sacred Head, now wounded,
with grief and shame weighed down,
now scornfully surrounded with thorns,
Thine only crown;
How pale Thou art with anguish,
with sore abuse and scorn!
How does that visage languish
which once was bright as morn!

Justification

Focus Verse:

*B*ut *God demonstrates His own love toward us, in that
while we were still sinners, Christ died for us. Much
more then, having now been justified by His blood, we shall
be saved from wrath through Him.*

-Romans 5:8-9

Greek: *Dikaiosis* (dik-ah-yo-sis) justification, acquittal (for
Christ's sake)

Theological Note:
Those whom God effectually calleth, He also freely
justifieth: not by infusing righteousness into them, but by
pardoning their sins, and by accounting and accepting their
persons as righteous; not for anything wrought in them, but
for Christ's sake alone; not by imputing faith itself, the act
of believing, or any other evangelical obedience to them, as
their righteousness; but by imputing the obedience and satisfaction of Christ unto them, they receiving and resting on
Him and His righteousness by faith; which faith they have
not of themselves, it is a gift of God.

-Westminster Confession

Pastoral Quote:

"It is entirely by the intervention of Christ's righteousness that we obtain justification before God. This is equivalent to saying that man is not just in himself, but that the righteousness of Christ is communicated to him by imputation, while he is strictly deserving of punishment."

-John Calvin

Reference Verses:

That having been justified by His grace we should become heirs according to the Hope of eternal life.

-Titus 3:7

Therefore, as through one man's offense judgment came to all men, resulting in condemnation, even so through one man's righteous act the free gift came to all men, resulting in justification of life.

-Romans 5:18

Galatians 2:16-20   Romans 4:25   I Corinthians 6:11

Quote:

"Tell me not of your justification, unless you have also some marks of sanctification. Boast not of Christ's work for you, unless you can show us the Spirit's work in you."

-John Charles (J.C.) Ryle
Anglican Bishop of
Liverpool, England
Pastor, scholar
(1816-1900)

Commentary:

The Reformers stood on the clear teaching of Scripture and declared that the doctrine of justification in Christ alone for salvation (*"Sola Fide"*) was a vital, non-negotiable doctrine of the true Church. Martin Luther went so far as to say that it was the doctrine on which the Church stands or falls. At the end of his life he challenged fellow ministers to preach the Gospel boldly and accurately, knowing it must be affirmed in every generation because of the constant attacks directed at this specific doctrine.

Luther was right. Man through the ages continuously attempts to subvert this doctrine by adding conditions to salvation. But human works and rituals, no matter how good or noble, can *never* justify us before God. We deserve only wrath and punishment for our sin and disobedience. Without Jesus, our attempts at righteousness are just filthy rags before God (Isa. 64:6).

Justification by faith in Christ alone is when we are placed in the mercy and grace of God. It is a judicial term meaning God, as Judge, declares forevermore that our faith in Jesus makes us righteous before Him, and all of our sin, past, present, and future is forgiven as He pardons and restores us. The only foundation of our justification is being cloaked in the righteousness of Christ.

It is clear in all of Scripture that sin is devastating, bringing condemnation and ultimately death. God hates sin and never views it as a small matter. Sin has created an enormous chasm between God and man. For us to be reconciled to Him, to no longer be an enemy of God, we have to be "made right" in His eyes. All have sinned and are in desperate need of deliverance and pardon. We owe a debt, because of our sin, we can never pay.

Justification is that moment in the salvation process that instantly delivers us from sin's penalty and condemnation into God's glorious forgiveness and life. God in that moment declares His verdict on our sin debt and proclaims that it is *paid in full* because of His Son's sacrifice. Our faith in the meritorious finished work of Christ cleanses and pardons us completely. When Abraham believed God, *"...He accounted it to him for righteousness"* (Gen. 15:6). In the same way God *imputes* Jesus' righteousness to us when we believe on His Son. It is Jesus' obedience, His perfection, the Father deems worthy. In the very moment we are justified by Christ we are forever in Him, and He is in us. The only righteousness that is acceptable to God is Jesus' righteousness.

We need to be reminded often that as Christians we are bought with a price. We do not own ourselves (I Cor. 6:19-20). Being justified in the eyes of God should make us aware that we are living our lives fully in His presence. The fact that Jesus is in us and we are in Him should prompt us to live in ongoing worship and thankfulness. A life that was once corrupted and bound by sin is now pardoned and free. How amazing the gift of Christ!

"For all have sinned and fall short of the glory of God, being justified freely by His grace through the redemption that is in Christ Jesus, whom God set forth as a propitiation by His blood through faith, to demonstrate His righteousness, because in His forbearance God had passed over the sins that were previously committed, to demonstrate at the present time His righteousness, that He might be just and the justifier of the one who has faith in Jesus."

-Romans 3:23-26

Historical Figure: *John Wesley*

Wesley was born June 8, 1703 in Epworth, England. He was an Anglican Cleric and Christian theologian who formed the Methodist movement. Wesley believed that each person could be saved by faith in God. Methodism was a highly successful evangelical movement in the United Kingdom, which encouraged people to experience Christ personally.

He was educated at Oxford where he became friends with the revivalist George Whitefield. Whitefield encouraged Wesley to not only preach in a chapel but to begin holding services outside for people who normally would not go to church. John eventually began holding revival services, (which the Anglican Church saw as controversial), and led thousands to Christ. He had a passionate heart for evangelism and living a holy, righteous life. His impact in Protestantism is far-reaching and he is still revered today for his place in Christian history. Wesley died in 1791.

Term: *"Imputation,"* to reckon to someone the blessing, curse or debt of another.
Example: our sins were *imputed* to Jesus, His righteousness was *imputed* to us.

Hymn: *"When I Survey the Wondrous Cross"*
   Words: Isaac Watts, 1707
   Music: Lowell Mason, 1824

When I survey the wondrous Cross
on which the Prince of glory died,
My richest gain I count but loss,
and pour contempt on all my pride. Amen

Life

Focus verse:

*A*nd the Lord God formed man of the dust of the ground, and breathed life into his nostrils the breath of life, and man became a living being.

-Genesis 2:7

Greek: *Zoe* (dzo-ay') life

Theological note:

God is the Author and Giver of all life. Only God has life independent of His creation. All other forms of life depend upon, and are sustained by God. Human life is sacred and no one has the right to murderously take it. The consumption and any misuse of blood is also prohibited because of its vital importance in all living beings (Leviticus 3:17). True life, which is eternal, can only be found in, and given by, Jesus Christ.

Pastoral quote:

"Men fail to see the miracle which God is working in every living thing."

-C.H. Spurgeon

Reference verses:

Then God said, "Let Us make Man in Our image, according to Our likeness."

-Genesis 1:26a

You shall not murder.

-Exodus 20:13

Deuteronomy 5:17   Leviticus 3:17
Matthew 4:4   James 4: 14-15

Quote:

"Ethics, too, are nothing but reverence for life. This is what gives me the fundamental principles of morality, namely, that God consists in maintaining, promoting, and enhancing life, and that destroying, injuring, and limiting life are evil."

-Albert Schweitzer
German physician,
theologian (1875-1965)

Commentary:

Human life is sacred. God is the Giver of all life and because of this truth every life is His possession. He is the One who breathes life into human beings and all living creatures. No one has the right to end human life because we are made in His image and likeness. God sustains and nurtures His creation. In Psalm 139:13-14 King David wrote these divinely inspired words, *"For You formed my inward parts; You covered me in my mother's womb. I will praise You for I am fearfully and wonderfully made; marvelous are Your works, and that my soul knows very well."* It is understood

Biblically that life begins at conception and that human life is precious and sacred to God.

In the Old Testament we see that Man is created in the image of God (Gen. 1:27). The theological term *Imago Dei* means we are made in, and bear, His image. This image bearing is given to humans alone, and no other living creature has this privilege and position. When Cain murders Abel it is Abel's blood that cries out to God declaring to humanity the sacredness of life and how God views the shedding of innocent blood. In Exodus 21 a death penalty is announced for all that violate God's mandate to preserve human life. In ordaining human government, God places the authority of the state over a society to protect its people and punish those who perform evil. This can include capital punishment (Rom. 13:4).

The shedding of animal blood in the Old Testament sacrificial system pointed to the sacred blood of Jesus who would one day shed His own blood and lay down His life to redeem us from sin (Lev. 17:11). The shedding of blood under this covenant with Israel was a gruesome reminder of the costly price of sin which always leads to death (Rom. 6:23).

In the New Testament we see a new covenantal relationship brought forth by the death and resurrection of Jesus Christ. Now His life is in us and we are in Him. We are made members of His Body (I Cor. 12:12) and are *born again* to new life and eternal fellowship with God (John 3:3). The sacredness of life is now more than Old Testament laws of protection but have become a command to respect and honor humanity with the law of love.

We are more than just flesh and blood. We carry within us the divine breath of God. We are eternal because being created in God's image means we are spirit as He is spirit (John 4:24). Animal life is not eternal, and though animals can exhibit personality they are not spiritual beings. Plant and insect life are also finite and do not possess any spiritual content. Those who argue that plants, animals, and insects have spiritual content hold to an unbiblical belief system called *animism* which is a tenet of pagan religions.

The historical Christian Church affirms through the centuries that as image bearers of God we are to uphold the sacredness, dignity, and value that is placed on each unique person. A person's dignity and value is not diminished because of a lack of ability, intelligence, dependency, mobility, size, or what he can or cannot produce. Our value certainly has nothing to do with the color of our skin. This profound value of human life is being eroded in our society as it embraces a culture of death. We have diminished and de-valued human life with the immergence and social acceptance of abortion, euthanasia, legalized physician-assisted suicide, and the push for human cloning.

As Christians we must stand for the weak and marginalized in our community and nation. We must also watch our own attitudes when we esteem someone higher than another because this can easily lead to class distinction, elitism, and social hierarchy even among believers (Phil. 2:3-4).

Our earthly life is quickly passing. James compares this life to a *"...vapor that appears for a moment and vanishes away"* (James 4:14). Jesus said, *"The thief (Satan) comes to kill, steal, and destroy, but I have come that they may have life, and that they may have it more abundantly"* (John 10:10). Even though our earthly life is fragile we have great importance to God. How we live and what we believe matters, for it is in this earthly existence that our eternal destiny, Heaven or Hell, is decided.

Ultimately *eternal life* for man is found only in Jesus Christ. This is the thrust of the Gospel and the reason we must proclaim Christ to all people and all nations. *The Great Commission* can be seen as a declaration of God's love toward humanity and the profound value He places on every individual human life (Matt. 28:16-20).

Historical Figure: *Moses*

Moses was the leader of the Israelites in their Exodus out of Egypt and during their 40 years of wilderness wandering as they journeyed to the Promised Land of Canaan. He was a great Israeli leader, lawgiver, and prophet who authored the first five books of the Bible called the *Pentateuch,* also called the *Torah*, or *The Law*. Moses received the Ten Commandments at Mount Sinai from God. He was a powerful man of God who was used to bring about a special relationship between the Hebrew people and God Himself. Moses is still esteemed as one of the most important men in Judeo-Christian history. He died in the wilderness and was buried by God. To this day we do not know where his burial place is located.

Term: *"Covenant,"* an agreement, pact or contract between two parties. The covenant, or testament, is a central theme throughout Scripture.

Hymn: *"Jesus, Keep Me Near The Cross"*
  Words: Fanny J. Crosby, 1869
  Music: William H. Doane, 1869

Jesus keep me near the cross,
there a precious fountain,
free to all a healing stream,
flows from Calvary's mountain,
In the cross, in the cross,
be my glory ever,
till my ransomed soul shall find,
rest beyond the river.

The Lord's Supper

Focus verse:

*A*nd as they were eating, Jesus took bread, blessed and broke it, and gave it to the disciples and said, "Take eat, this is My body." Then He took the cup, and gave thanks, and gave it to them, saying, "Drink from it, all of you. For this is My blood of the new covenant, which is shed for many for the remissions of sins."

-Matthew 26:26-27

Greek: The apostle Paul used the term *"koinonia"* to describe the nature of the Lord's Supper which expresses the core meaning of the Christian Faith. A sharing in the life and death of Jesus Christ. The Greek *"koinonia"* means communion, fellowship, and sharing in common.

Theological note:

The Lord's Supper is an ordinance of Jesus Christ, to be administered with the elements of bread and wine, and to be observed by the churches till the end of the world. It is in no sense a sacrifice, but is designed to commemorate His death, to confirm the faith and other graces of Christians, and to be

a bond, pledge and renewal of their communion with Him, and of their church fellowship.
                    -Southern Baptist Theological Seminary, 1858

Pastoral Quote:

"It is not a converting ordinance, or a saving ordinance; it is an establishing ordinance and a comforting ordinance for those who are saved. What does this supper mean? It means communion. Communion with Christ, communion with one another."
                    -Charles Haddon Spurgeon

Reference verses:

Therefore whoever eats this bread or drinks this cup of the Lord in an unworthy manner will be guilty of the body and blood of the Lord. But let a man examine himself and so let him eat of the bread and drink the cup. For he who eats and drinks in an unworthy manner eats and drinks judgment to himself, not discerning the Lord's body.
                    -I Corinthians 11:27-29

And Jesus said to them, "I am the Bread of Life. He who comes to Me shall never hunger, and he who believes in Me shall never thirst."
                    -John 6:35

Luke 22:17-20   Mark 14:22-25

Quote:

"Our Lord Jesus, in the night wherein He was betrayed, instituted the sacrament of His body and blood, called the

Lord's Supper, to be observed in His Church, unto the end of the world, for the perpetual remembrance of the sacrifice of Himself in His death."

-Westminster Confession, 1646

Commentary:

The Lord's Supper is a ceremonial meal that believers share to commemorate the death of Jesus Christ for our sin. It is one of two of the ordinances of Christianity, the other being baptism. The form of this ordinance was established by Jesus at the Last Supper when He offered Himself as the sacrificial Lamb of atonement. His death on the cross the next day fulfilled His prophetic words and brought the only means of salvation to the world.

Jesus instituted this ordinance during the Passover meal. The Passover feast was part of the Passover Festival when Israel celebrated their deliverance from Egypt. Jesus now establishes a new covenant with His sacrifice on the cross that will bring deliverance from the bondage of sin for all mankind. This reveals the continuity of redemption throughout both old and new covenants.

Paul uses the term *"Lord's Supper"* (I Cor.11:20). Early church fathers after 100 A.D. also began calling it the *"Eucharist"* which means "thanksgiving." It is also commonly called *"Communion"* and *"The Lord's Table."*

This sacrament is performed by the believer taking the bread and the wine (many churches use grape juice) and while eating and drinking they remember what Jesus did for them on the cross. It is also a time we express our faith in Him publicly, and look forward to His return. This time of corporate worship and remembrance is found in all Christian churches in some form throughout the world.

The Reformers rejected the Catholic Church's doctrine of "transubstantiation" (conversion of one substance into another), where Catholics believe as they take the bread and the wine during Mass they are actually miraculously partaking of Jesus' flesh and blood. Catholic theology says that at the Catholic Mass, Jesus' sacrifice on the cross is repeated and renewed. The problem with that teaching is that the Mass ritual obscures the sufficiency of Jesus' *once and for all* atoning death (II Cor. 5:14-15).

The Reformers affirmed the belief of the early church fathers and insisted that at the Lord's Supper all we are doing is giving thanks for the sufficient, finished, and accepted work of Christ's atonement. The Lord's Supper as *symbolism is the* orthodox (accepted) view of the historical New Testament church.

Church fellowships regularly celebrate this ordinance as a sign of the *new covenant* sealed by Christ's death and resurrection. The Lord's Supper communicates visibly what is heard in the Gospel. It can be a very powerful time of corporate worship, unity, repentance, and celebration as together we remember Jesus' amazing love and grace towards us. It is also a continual reminder that He is certainly coming again.

Historical Figure: *Polycarp*

Polycarp of Smyrna lived between 70 A.D. and 155 A.D. which connects him to the first century church and the early church fathers. He was a direct pupil of the *Apostle John*. Polycarp was a bishop of the church in Smyrna, the "persecuted church." When he was arrested for being a Christian by the Roman proconsul he was told to denounce Christ and say that "Caesar is Lord," and in doing so he would escape torture and death. Polycarp replied, *"86 years I have served Christ, and He never did me wrong. How can I blaspheme my King who saved me?"* He was then stabbed and burned to death at the stake. Polycarp was an early defender of the Faith and fought the Gnostic heresies of his day. His sole surviving work is his letter to the Philippians. His famous pupil was Irenaeus. Polycarp's martyrdom has been a source of courage throughout the centuries for persecuted believers standing for the truth of Jesus Christ.

Term: *"Dialectic,"* the practice of examining ideas, theories, and beliefs using reason and logic.

Hymn: *"Here At Thy Table, Lord"*
  Words: May P. Hoyt
  Music: *Bread of Life*, William F. Sherwin, 1877

Here at Thy table Lord, this sacred hour,
O let us feel Thee near, in loving power;
calling our thoughts away, from self and sin,
as to Thy banquet hall we enter in.

Love

Focus verse:

A new commandment I give to you, that you love one another; as I have loved you, that you also love one another. By this all will know that you are My disciples, if you have love for one another.

-John 13: 34-35

<u>Greek</u>: *Agape* (ag-ah'-pay) benevolence, charity, Divine love

 Phileo (fil-eh'-o) to be a friend, affection

<u>Theological note:</u>

Love is a commitment that holds in high regard the benefit, value, and well-being of another person. I Corinthians 13:4-8a defines God's view of love: *"Love suffers long and is kind; love does not envy, love does not parade itself, is not puffed up; does not behave rudely, does not seek it's own, is not provoked, thinks no evil, does not rejoice in iniquity, but rejoices in the truth; bears all things, hopes all things, endures all things. Love never fails."* Love originates in the heart of God, for God is love.

Pastoral quote:

"Our Lord told His disciples that love and obedience were organically united. The final test of love is obedience."
-Aiden Wilson (A.W.) Tozer
American pastor, author
(1897-1963)

Reference verses:

Now hope does not disappoint, because the love of God has been poured out in our hearts by the Holy Spirit who was given to us.
-Romans 5:5

We know that we have passed from death to life, because we love the Brethern. He who does not love his brother abides in death. Whoever hates his brother is a murderer, and you know that no murderer has eternal life abiding in him. By this we know we love, because He laid down His life for us. And we also ought to lay down our lives for the Brethern.
- I John 3:14-16

Romans 12:9-19   John 3:16-17
I Corinthians 13:1-13   Galatians 5:14
John 15:13 Luke 6:27

Quote:

"You can give without loving. But you cannot love without giving."
-Amy Carmichael
Irish missionary to India
(1867-1951)

Commentary:

Love is a *commitment*, not a *feeling*. True love is not seeking what another person can do for you, that is selfishness. It is not about physical pleasure, for that is lust. When we realize this truth it will revolutionize the way we view our relationships with God, family, friends, strangers, and even our enemies. We must also understand that love is an attribute of God and our capacity to love others is given by Him (Rom. 5:8). Jesus said the world would know we are His people because of the distinct way we love. This Christ centered love is unconditional and hopeful. Our faith in Christ produces true love through the Holy Spirit living within the believer. This Godly love is transforming in its power to literally change the human heart.

We are consumed by a romantic notion of love in our nation. This fairytale mentality says, *"I will be happy if I can only find my soul-mate and fall in love. He/She will meet my deepest needs and we will live happily ever after."* This imaginary concept of love produces a conditional, fickle relationship that is based on emotional needs and physical pleasure. This false love vanishes when the object of your desire fails you. One thing is for certain: people will let you down. Real love is when you stand within that pain and confusion and refuse to cast them aside. True love says, *"I will endure, I will sacrifice, I will care even if I get nothing from you in return."*

Jesus changed the way we perceive love when He said we are to love our enemies. This was a radical idea in the ancient Church and remains so today. It is against our human nature to put others before ourselves. Certainly it seems impossible to the average person to care for someone who actively persecutes and hates them. Jesus said anyone could love those who also love them, but it was only through God that we could see beyond the darkness of sin and see our persecutor as someone in need of the hope and love of Christ.

In the Sermon on the Mount (Matt.ch. 5-7) Jesus teaches what the law could only point to (Rom. 13:10). He brings to the world this truth that reveals the heart and purposes of God. He would later put in full display the magnitude of His words when He hung on the cross, crucified by His enemies and cried, *"Father forgive them, for they know not what they do."* This amazing plea from the sinless Son to His Father forever established a new way to deal with those who hate us. The cross also was the defining moment that God's people embraced fully that love costs, and true love is sacrificial.

The Bible teaches that we are never to seek vengeance when we are wronged. This is what Christ meant when He said, *"Turn the other cheek"* (Matt 5:39). God is clear in His Word that *"Vengeance is Mine, I shall repay"* (Rom 12:19b). When we pray for, and forgive those who have hurt us, we are then set free to love them. We know that God will judge them according to His will and in His timing. His rebuke will be fair and sufficient, whereas our revenge can easily be far beyond what God would deem as appropriate. We also benefit by not carrying hatred and bitterness in our hearts which always hurts us more than the one who wronged us. Often people who have hurt others will seek reconciliation because they were forgiven and shown love. True forgiveness stems from God's love and grace which says to our offender, "You no longer owe me anything, I will hold nothing against you."

The Greek word *"agape"* is used to designate unconditional Godly love. This agape love of God is how we are called and empowered to walk in love. This self-giving love is a picture of Christ as Servant. Only in His love can we transcend the lust and greed of the fallen nature of man. The Apostle Paul, in his great discourse on love in First Corinthians chapter 13, says it beautifully: *"...love bears all things, believes all things, hopes all things, endures all things. Love never fails."* It is this kind of selfless love that should characterize the individual Christian and the Church as a whole. We are *commanded* to love other Christians. This directive from Jesus takes our emotions out of the equation. The only way to do this is to consciously submit our will to Christ and prayerfully allow Him to bring a servant mindset towards fellow Christians that we have disagreements, prejudices or difficulties with.

It is love that will endure for all eternity after the earthly need for faith and hope passes away. That is why the Bible states that love is the greatest of these three. *God is love.* May we love Him with our whole heart, mind, body and soul. May we be quick to love and quick to forgive. We should always stand amazed in the knowledge that *Jesus first loved us*...and His love never fails!

"In this the love of God was manifested toward us, that God has sent His only begotten Son into the world, that we might live through Him. In this is love, not that we loved God, but that He loved us and sent His Son to be the propitiation for our sins. Beloved, if God so loved us, we also ought to love one another."

-I John 4:9-11

Historical Figure: *Henry Martyn*

Henry Martyn was born on February 18, 1781. He was an Anglican priest and missionary to the people of India and Persia. Martyn was a brilliant theologian educated at St. John's College, Cambridge. He was ordained a priest in the Church of England and became a Chaplain for the British East India Company. He is an important figure in Christian history in the realm of theology and missions. He died in 1812.

Term: *"Syncretism,"* The assimilation of one religion's beliefs and practices into another. This concept attempts to

unify some, or all, religious systems. This idea always compromises the Christian Faith and subverts the Word of God.

Hymn: *"Love Lifted Me"*
      Words: James Rowe, 1912
      Music: Howard E. Smith, 1912

I was sinking deep in sin,
far from the peaceful shore,
very deeply stained within,
sinking to rise no more;
but the Master of the sea,
heard my despairing cry,
from the waters lifted me
now safe am I,
Love lifted me, love lifted me,
when nothing else
could help, love lifted me.

Marriage

Focus verse:

*T*herefore a man shall leave his father and mother and be joined to his wife, and they shall become one flesh.

-Genesis 2:24

Greek: *Gamos* (gam'os) nuptials, marriage

Theological Note:

Marriage was ordained for the mutual help of husband and wife, for the increase of mankind with a legitimate issue, and of the church with a holy seed; and preventing of uncleanness (sexual immorality).

–Westminster Confession

Pastoral Quote:

"Eve was not taken out of Adam's head to be above him, neither out of his feet to be trampled by him, but out of his side to be equal with him, under his arm to be protected by him, and near his heart to be loved by him."

–Matthew Henry

Reference Verses:

Marriage is honorable among all, and the bed undefiled; but fornicators and adulterers God will judge.
-Hebrew 13:4

It is good for a man not to touch a woman. Nevertheless, because of sexual immorality, let each man have his own wife, and let each woman have her own husband.
-I Corinthians 7:1-2

I Corinthians 7:10-16   Malachi 2:16
Matthew 19:3-6 I Corinthians 7:39

Quote:

"There is no more lovely, friendly or charming relationship, communion or company, than a good marriage."
-Martin Luther

Commentary:

The Bible teaches that marriage is a divine institution. It is a monogamous, unconditional relationship between a man and a woman. God's standard for this relationship is that it be for a lifetime and built on the foundation of His unconditional love for us. This "one flesh" marriage commitment is only second to our commitment to God. It is to be protected and held above all other earthly relationships including our parents and our children.

Christian marriage is based on the greater mystery and fellowship of Jesus' relationship with the Church, the Bride of Christ. The earthly *temporary* institution of matrimony (there will be no marriage in Heaven, Matt. 22:30), symbolizes the *eternal* relationship between Christ and His Church (Ephesians 5: 21-33). No longer is God unapproachable as in the days of the Old Testament but now in Christ we are one with Him (Gal. 3:28).

As Christ submitted to the Father's will and laid down His life for us, husbands are called to lay their lives down for their wives. This concept of *submission* does not mean that the woman is less than the man. It means that the husband is the head of the home as Christ is the Head of the Church. The husband deserves the respect of the wife but should never rule over her or oppress her. He is to serve her and take care of her needs, loving her unconditionally and faithfully. He is to monetarily provide for her and bring physical and spiritual protection to the family. The wife in turn, through Godly submission, serves her husband by showing him the respect he deserves, expressing love, companionship, and faithfulness as she provides a home full of grace and tenderness.

Does submission mean that the wife has to do everything the husband tells her to do? Not necessarily. In Ephesians 5:22 the Bible says a wife submits to the husband *"as is to the Lord."* If a husband asks his wife to violate the will of God or do something illegal or illicit, the wife is to first honor God and is not bound to the husband's request. If a husband is submitted to God he will not demand sinful behavior, or illicit submission from his wife. As marriage partners, spouses should always feel free to bring their concerns, needs and expectations to one another. Both the man and the woman have equal dignity and value but differing roles within the family structure, and should show mutual respect for those roles.

Marriage is a gift from God to build Christ-centered families and to transfer our Faith to the next generation. It is in the context of marriage that sexual relations are permitted by God. This sexual union brings oneness to the married couple that God deems holy and binding. The sexual union is God's good gift to us for the expressing of our love to one another, building intimacy within the marriage, and for procreation.

This is why adultery and any other sexual sin outside of the marriage bond is seen by God as devastating and unholy (I Cor. 6:12-20). Sex outside of marriage defiles the purity of the marriage bed, breaking the oneness of the couple, and destroying trust. This betrayal often leads to divorce and the intense pain of family separation.

True love is not a *feeling*, it is a *commitment*. Marriage cannot be based on how we feel about our spouse from day to day. Human emotions can be fickle and sporadic. If our relationship is built on feelings we can easily pull away and begin to isolate from our mate. Our commitment to God and the solemn vows we take before Him must be the foundation of a lifelong marriage commitment. Family prayer and Bible study in the home can be a tremendous way to solidify the marriage covenant and maintain intimacy. It is also a great way to focus your family's purpose while encouraging communication and participation from all family members in the home.

It is clear that a Christian should never enter into a marriage with an unbeliever (II Cor. 6:14). If you are saved after marriage and your spouse remains an unbeliever you are to stay with them as a witness unless they ask to depart from the marriage. I Corinthians chapter 7 outlines the basic principles of Christian marriage.

When we see the awesome love that compelled Jesus to sacrificially commit to us as His Church we should be ever aware of how seriously He takes the marriage vows. Let Christ's love inform how we view earthly marriage. This divine institution is never to be made something profane, illicit, or entered into lightly. A loving Christian family is a very powerful witness for Christ on earth.

Historical Figure: *John Bunyan*

John Bunyan was born on November 28, 1628 in Elstow, England. He was an English Christian writer and non-conformist preacher, famous for writing *"The Pilgrim's Progress,"* arguably the most famous Christian allegory in history. He wrote several other books including *"Grace Abounding."* Bunyan was imprisoned for preaching the Gospel several times, and became a popular and influential leader of the non-conformist movement throughout England. He died in 1688.

<u>**Term:**</u> *"Gnosticism,"* *"gnosis"* means knowledge. The Gnostics in the first century believed "special knowledge" led to salvation. This heretical teaching declared that Jesus was not the Incarnate Son of God and His death on the cross was not sufficient for the atonement of man's sin.

<u>**Hymn:**</u> *"Leaning On The Everlasting Arms"*
   Words: Elisha A. Hoffman, 1887
   Music: Anthony J. Showalter, 1887

What a fellowship, what a joy divine,
Leaning on the everlasting arms;
What a blessedness what a peace is mine,
Leaning on the everlasting arms.
Leaning, leaning, safe and secure from all alarms,
Leaning, leaning on Jesus, leaning on the everlasting arms.

Missions

Focus verse:

*A*nd Jesus came to them saying, "All the authority has been given to Me in Heaven and on earth. Go therefore and make disciples of all nations, baptizing them in the name of the Father, and of the Son, and of the Holy Spirit, teaching them to observe all things that I have commanded you: and lo I am with you always, even to the end of the age." Amen.

-Matthew 28:18-20

Greek: The word *mission* (or *missionary*) is not found in Scripture, but the concept of missions is seen throughout the Word of God.

Theological Note:

A task given by God to go to people groups that have not yet heard the Gospel of Jesus Christ. The person called to this specific ministry is known as a missionary. They are set apart to fulfill the Great Commission by going into other nations or un-reached domestic areas, and through the power of Christ, producing Christian converts through the preaching of the Word, church planting, and various discipleship and evangelism methods.

Pastoral Quote:

"The Spirit of Christ is the spirit of missions. The nearer we get to Him, the more intensely missionary we become."
–Henry Martyn
British Anglican minister
Missionary to India
(1781-1812)

Reference Verses:

For the Son of Man has come to seek and to save that which was lost.
-Luke 19:10

For God so loved the world that He gave His only begotten Son, that whoever believes in Him should not perish but have everlasting life. For God did not send His Son into the world to condemn the world but that the world through Him might be saved.
-John 3:16-17
John 1:18 John 13:31
Acts 1-8 (Jerusalem) Acts 8- 12
Samaria) Acts 13-28 (World)

Quote:

"If a commission by an earthly king is considered an honor, how can a commission from a Heavenly King be considered a sacrifice?"
-Dr. David Livingstone
Scottish medical missionary,
explorer (1813-1873)

"Not called, did you say? 'Not heard the call,' I think you should say. Put your ear down to the Bible, and hear Jesus bid you go and pull sinners out of the fire of sin. Put your ear down to the burdened, agonized heart of humanity, and listen to its pitiful wail for help. Go stand by the gates of Hell, and hear the damned entreat you to go to their father's house and bid their brother's and sister's not to come there. Then look at Christ in the face — whose mercy you have professed to obey — and tell Him whether you will join heart, soul, body and circumstances in the march to publish His mercy to the world."

-William Booth
British Methodist minister
Founder, Salvation Army
(1829-1912)

Commentary:

We get our word *mission* from the Latin word *"missio"* which means *"to send."* A missionary is one who is called by God to take the Gospel of Jesus Christ to a certain group of people. Missions originated within the heart of God, for He is the missionary God. The Bible reveals the awesome mission that began in Heaven when God sent His Son Jesus to *"seek and to save that which was lost"* (Luke 19:10).

Throughout Jesus' teachings to His disciples He made it clear that the mission to reach the lost with the Gospel was to continue until He returns, and with the aid of the Holy Spirit it would be a powerful and fruitful mission (I Cor. 2:1-5). It is clear in Christ's *Great Commission* that the mission of the church is to go into all nations, tribes, ethnic groups, social classes, and cultures (Matt. 28:18-20). It was the intent of Jesus that the Church would continually reach out beyond itself. This "mission mindedness" is the fuel, the lifeblood of the church.

This call to missions is from God alone. The Church has the great privilege of preaching the Gospel and leading people to Christ, participating in the *Missio Dei, "the sending of God."* But be assured, missions is for the purpose of God on earth for His glorification, and to fulfill His Word from the beginning to restore fallen man to Himself.

Today the mission of the Church, through the leading of the Holy Spirit (Acts 13:2-4), is still to send missionaries to all parts of the world and preach and teach the Word in every nation. Planting churches in specific areas is another primary focus of missions. Missionaries take on the vital task of discipling and training local converts to take on leadership roles in those church plants and providing them spiritual, administrative, and financial direction until the church is a self-supported fellowship.

The Apostle Paul was the first missionary. He was sent to the Gentiles (anyone who is not a Jew) to preach the Gospel (Acts 26:16-18). God has used his example as an evangelist and church planter for 2,000 years to ignite a passion for the lost within the Church. In the past 125 years there has been an explosion of missionary agencies formed to help support local fellowships in equipping and supporting missionaries for service domestically and internationally. A "short term" mission trip (working with missionaries for a few weeks or months) is a great way to assist fulltime missionaries on the field and to see how this ministry branch of the Church functions.

Missionaries on the mission field today are selflessly giving their lives for the proclamation of the Gospel and discipling new believers throughout the world. Sometimes we think to be "on mission" we must go to another country, but we must realize we are all called to share the Truth in love here and abroad. You may find yourself carrying the *Good News* to people on the other side of the world or maybe across the street in your neighborhood. Either way, God has placed you there to fulfill His mandate to proclaim the Lord Jesus. Wherever we may find ourselves at this time in history we are to be faithful to share the love and hope of Christ to all those who are still in darkness.

Historical Figure: *Lottie Moon*

Charlotte Digges "Lottie" Moon was born on December 12, 1840 in Virginia. She was a Southern Baptist missionary to China with the Foreign Mission Board who spent nearly 40 years ministering to the Chinese people. As a teacher and evangelist she laid a foundation for solid support for missions among Baptists in America. She is seen as one of the most selfless and important missionaries in history. The SBC honors her memory each year with *"The Lottie Moon Christmas Offering"* which is used to fund overseas missionaries. She died on December 24, 1912.

Term: *"Dispensation,"* a ministry, stewardship or administration that God ordains for His purpose on earth. A divine ordering of the affairs of the world.

Hymn: *"Rescue the Perishing"*
Words: Fanny J. Crosby, 1869
Music: William H. Doane, 1869

Rescue the perishing, care for the dying,
snatch them in pity from sin and the grave;
Weep o'er the erring one, Lift up the fallen,
tell them of Jesus the mighty to save.
Rescue the perishing, care for the dying;
Jesus is merciful, Jesus will save.

Perseverance of the Saints

Focus verse:

P raying always with all prayer and supplication in the Spirit, being watchful to this end with all persever- ance and supplication for all saints.

-Ephesians 6:18

Greek: *Proskarteresis* (pros-kar-ter'-ay-sis) persistent, perseverance

Theological note:
Those whom God hath accepted in the Beloved, and sancti- fied by His Spirit, will never totally nor finally fall away from the state of grace, but shall certainly persevere to the end; and though they may fall through neglect and temptation into sin, whereby they grieve the Spirit, impair their graces and com- forts, bring reproach on the Church, temporal judgments on themselves, yet they shall be renewed again unto repentance, and be kept by the power of God through faith unto salvation.

-Southern Baptist Theological Seminary, 1858

Pastor quote:

"Those who fall away have never been thoroughly imbued with the knowledge of Christ but only had a slight and passing taste of it."

-John Calvin

Reference verses:

And I give them eternal life and they shall never perish; neither shall anyone snatch them out of My hand. My Father who has given them to Me is greater than all; and no one is able to snatch them out of My Father's hand. I and the Father are One.

-John 10:28-29

For I know whom I have believed and am persuaded that He is able to keep what I have committed to Him until that Day.

-II Timothy 1:12b

Romans 8:31-39   II Timothy 4:18
I Thessalonians 5:23 Hebrews 10: 35-39

Quote:

"Difficulties afford opportunities for learning God's faithfulness which otherwise we should not have. It gives me great comfort to remember that the work is His and that He knows how best to carry on and is infinitely more interested in it than we are."

-Hudson Taylor

Commentary:

Perseverance of the Saints is a doctrine of Christianity that is also known as *Eternal Security,* and the *Security of the Believer.* Sometimes referred to as *"once saved, always saved."* This doctrine teaches that one who is saved will continue in the Faith and not fall away. The fearful question that haunts many people is, *"Can I lose my salvation because of certain sins or temporarily doubting my faith in Christ?"* For the answer to this question we need only examine the Word of God to find the truth.

Our salvation depends on God's power to establish it. My sin cannot defeat the will of the Lord and His sovereign purpose for my life if I am redeemed by Christ.

"So He is able to save completely those who come to God through Him, because He lives to ever intercede for them" (Hebrews 7:25). The key word is *completely.* A Christian at conversion becomes a new creation in Jesus Christ. We are then indwelled by the Holy Spirit and have become the temple of God (I Cor. 6:19-20). Jesus said we are *in* Him and He is *in* us (John 15:5). This is the union that happens when we are baptized by the Holy Spirit at the moment of conversion. If we can fall away after being truly saved this would mean that the Body of Christ can be destroyed. This is simply not so.

"If God is for me, who can be against me?" (Rom. 8:31). The reality of this verse is that as a Christian *I* cannot even be against *me.* If God accepts me and redeems me through the faith I have placed in His Son, He secures me for eternity. I am now placed in His hands, being held by Almighty God. *"I give them eternal life, and they shall never perish; neither shall anyone snatch them out of My hand"* (John 10:28).

My failures and doubts in this quickly passing life cannot destroy the eternal grip that Christ has on my soul. If my sin, as a Christian, can abolish my freedom and salvation in

Jesus, then my sin becomes greater and more powerful than the promises of God. This is absurd. *I cannot lose my salvation because God cannot lose me.* I am His, He is mine. I have become a child of God. I cannot lose that designation if my salvation experience was genuine no matter the level of my daily faith or maturity throughout the seasons of my life.

The fear of losing one's salvation is perpetuated by the wrong assumption of some that after conversion a Christian no longer sins. So when Christians do sin and wander away from a daily obedient walk with Christ, it raises questions in some fellow believer's minds, especially those prone to legalism and being overly judgmental. This overt sinful behavior may cast doubts about that person's faith and cause some to believe the guilty person has "lost" their salvation. On the other hand, Christians who are involved in blatant sin can *feel* that they are no longer saved during and after a season of rebellion, especially if they view their salvation with a "works" mindset.

People who say that Christians can lose their salvation because of sinful behavior find it difficult to deal with this issue of a believer's sin nature. I John 3:6 states, ***"Whoever abides in Him does not sin. He who sins has neither seen Him nor known Him."*** They will take a verse like this and use it as a proof text that you can't be a Christian if you sin, or you lose your salvation at some point when you do sin. But this thinking logically produces the question: *"At what point do we actually lose our salvation?"* What line must be crossed? How much sin does it take? This "score keeping" type of faith is certainly exhausting and in the end counter productive, fearful, and guilt based.

The truth is we must read that particular scripture in context with everything else the Apostle John is teaching the Church, and the whole of the Bible. He is not saying Christians are incapable of sinning. The Bible is clear that as believers we still battle our flesh (Rom. ch. 7). The reality is that when one is born again they now have *two* natures; the old nature/flesh and the new nature/spirit. The old nature is now seen by God as set aside in the death of Christ, and the new nature born of God cannot sin (though the old nature can still manifest sin in this earthly life). Sin's reign over us is defeated because we are no longer slaves to sin, having a new master in Christ. But we can still certainly commit sins of commission (willfully doing wrong) and omission (not doing what we know is right) as Christians in our day to day lives (Rom. 6: 6-14).

Saying we are sinless is actually a sin because only God is perfect. We are *sinners* saved by grace, justified only because of Jesus' righteousness. What John is saying is that Christians are to submit to a higher standard (Jesus Christ), and that sin should not be habitual, frequent, or justified in the life of a believer. As a Christian willfully sins, his communion and joy with Christ may be lost for a season, yet the fundamental relationship stays in tact; Father/child, Savior/redeemed. For example: a son rebels against his earthly father and harms their relationship, but the son can never lose the designation of being the father's biological child no matter what he has done.

People who make a public commitment to Christ and then fall away and <u>deny</u> the Faith were *never truly saved* to begin with. They may have walked as a Christian, and for a time played the church "game," did some good works, and were emotionally fulfilled, but they were never *indwelled* by the Holy Spirit. They may have had a cathartic emotional experience but it was not a *conversion* experience. The Parable of the Sower in Matthew chapter 13 (those who fall away are the *second hearers* of the Word, v. 20-21) reveals the truth of how people respond to the Gospel, and helps us flesh out this sometimes troubling and confusing aspect of spiritual conversion or rejection.

John previously said to *believers* in I John 1:8-9, *"If we say we have no sin, we deceive ourselves, and the truth is not in us. If we confess our sin He is faithful and just to forgive our sins and to cleanse us from all unrighteousness."* Again, John is clearly saying that Christians can sin and even fall into gross immorality (such as some of the Corinthian believers, I Cor. ch. 5). The promise is that if we confess our sin and repent, no matter the degree of our sin, God will restore us to a fruitful and joyous relationship with Christ. *That is grace.* God's grace is not fickle or shallow; it is a permanent fixture of the Christian life.

We see throughout the Bible that men of God failed miserably. King David, *"a man after God's own heart,"* committed adultery, murder, and sins of lust, anger and pride. He was forgiven but he also had to bear the severe consequences of his sin. Peter is another glaring example of a man transformed by Jesus and then sadly failing Him early in his faith. Paul even claimed that he himself was the *chief of sinners* (I Tim. 1:15). In the same way, we as Christians cannot lose our salvation because of sin, but we can experience painful consequences for our rebellion. We should not test God in this area. Instead we should strive to be Christ-like, yielding to the Holy Spirit within us, repentant, and thankful.

Continued sin in the life of a believer will bear sorrow, fruitlessness, loss of testimony, and certain discipline from God. *"And do not grieve the Holy Spirit of God, by whom you were sealed for the day of redemption"* (Eph. 4:30). As Christians we are forever safe in the power of Jesus' salvation, but we are warned in this Scripture passage to live a holy life and shun sin. This warning is not to withhold pleasure from us, but to actually bring us into the fullness and joy of living out a faithful daily walk with Christ.

God sees the big picture of our lives, not just the moments of failure and doubt, or even moments of victory. He has promised to keep us and grow us into the likeness of Christ. This is

His purpose and *He* will fulfill it. If you have placed your faith in Christ and accepted Jesus as your Lord and Savior, you can never be lost again.

We will persevere in the Faith not because of the strength of our commitment to Christ but because of the power of His commitment to us. The Holy Spirit within us is God's promise of ultimate redemption. Once you are saved you are forever sealed by The Holy Spirit and secured by the love of Christ. God will give you the strength and grace to persevere in the Faith until He calls you home.

"For I am persuaded that neither death nor life, nor angels nor principalities nor powers, nor things present nor things to come, nor height nor depth, nor any other created thing, shall be able to separate me from the love of God, which is in Christ Jesus our Lord."

-Romans 8:38-39

Historical Figure: *Richard Wurmbrand*

Wurmbrand was born on March 24, 1909 in Bucharest. He was a Romanian evangelical Christian minister, author and educator who spent a total of 14 years imprisoned in Romania for preaching the Gospel and distributing Bibles. He was the founder of the *Voice of the Martyrs*, a missions and relief agency that assists, and brings attention to, the worldwide persecuted Church. His work within the persecuted Christian community has been a tremendous blessing worldwide and has brought much needed attention to the modern day suffering of the Church. He died on February 17, 2001.

Term: *"Agnostic,"* "a" meaning *no*, and "gnosis" meaning *knowledge*. The belief that you cannot know there is, or is not, a God.

<u>Hymn:</u> *"How Firm A Foundation"*
Words: John Rippon, *"Selection of Hymns,"* 1787
Music: Joseph Funk, *"Genuine Church Music,"* 1832

How firm a foundation,
ye saints of the Lord,
is laid for your faith in
His excellent Word,
what more can He say
than to you He hath said,
to you for refuge to Jesus have fled?

Prayer

Focus verse:

B *e anxious for nothing, but in everything by prayer and supplication, with thanksgiving, let your requests be known to God.*

-Philippians 4:6

Greek: *Proseuchomai*: (pros-yoo'-khom-ahee) praying to God, supplication, active worship

Theological Note:
   In the Bible, prayer is directed to God the Father through the name of Jesus the Son, and is interpreted and interceded by the Holy Spirit. Prayer is impossible without the help of the Holy Spirit (Romans 8:26-28). Faith is essential to our prayer life. Supplication is seen as an inferior making a request of a superior.

✳ someone small asking something
   of someone above them (me → God)

Pastoral Quote:

"Do not have your concert first and then tune your instruments afterwards. Begin the day with the Word of God and prayer, and go first of all into harmony with Him."
-Hudson Taylor
English missionary
to China (1832-1905)

Reference verses:

And all things, whatsoever you shall ask in prayer, believing, you shall receive.
-Matthew 21:22

Call unto Me, and I will answer thee, and show thee great and mighty things, which thou knowest not.
-Jeremiah 33:3

Matthew 7:7-8   I John 5:14-15   Psalm 50:15
Mark 11:24   John 15:7

Quote:
"And Satan trembles when he sees, the weakest saint upon his knees."
-William Cowper
Poet, Hymnist
(1731-1800)

Commentary:
In Matthew chapter 6 verses 5 through 14, Jesus gives us the *"Model Prayer."* This was not given to be empty recitation but given to show us what is important to bring to the Father in prayer. Jesus is clear that our motives for praying must be pure. Our motives will also determine how we pray

and what we pray for. As we mature in our relationship with Christ our prayer requests will be more and more in tune with His will, not ours.

The model prayer has six requests. Three for the Kingdom of God to come and three asking God to meet our needs according to His grace and mercy. Jesus says that the Father's name is hallowed. Not only is God's name holy and should never be used profanely (to be made common), it implies that He is the Majestic King above all kings who will insure our eternity in Heaven.

Prayer is a discipline. Do not let this scare you away. It is a privilege to come boldly to the throne of God through Jesus, and an amazing truth that we have direct access to God Almighty, that He hears and answers us when we call.

Where do we start this journey of prayer? Here are a few simple suggestions to get you moving. Pray the Word back to God. Simply open the Psalms, and pick one or two passages daily as part of your prayer life. Also pray for God's Kingdom to be known throughout the earth, and that He would empower you to be salt and light to those around you (Matt. 5:13-14).

God will answer prayer in His timing and in His will. That means His answer to your prayers can be *yes, no, or wait*. Be specific with your requests. In painful circumstances ask Him to comfort and teach you through the hurt and suffering. Remember, He is your Heavenly Father who adores you, and desires to give you good things and an abundant life in Jesus Christ.

Praise the Lord for His faithfulness and provision with a thankful heart. Ask for forgiveness of sin and to help you deal with, and forgive, those who have hurt you. Ask Him to specifically meet needs in your life, family, church and nation. Seek to know Jesus and love Him more fully. Certainly pray for those who are lost that they would be saved. *Intercessory* prayer is when we pray for others. Starting a Scripture and prayer journal is a good way to hold yourself accountable in this area as you grow in Christ.

When you get married pray with your spouse daily for a few minutes, or set aside a family prayer time sometime during the week. The most intimate thing you will ever do with another person is pray together. Churches that make a special effort to have a time of sincere "altar prayer" in the weekly service seem to have a special unity and anointing. Let prayer be a foundational discipline for you, your spouse, and children as the years unfold.

You can pray anywhere, at anytime. Speak to God as you would to your closest friend, always keeping in mind that Jesus intercedes for you. Time spent in prayer to your Heavenly Father is life changing and will be a profound blessing that flows into every part of your life and surrounding relationships.

"The effective, fervent prayer of a righteous man avails much."

-James 5:16

Historical Figure: *Susanna Wesley*

John Wesley's mother, Susanna was born in January of 1669 and died July 23, 1742. Even though she never preached a sermon, established a church, or published a book, she is still known as the Mother of Methodism. Her two sons, Charles and John Wesley, applied their mother's teachings and example to their own ministries later in life. Her prayer time with her children deeply influenced John and Charles and was pivotal in promoting a disciplined faith that under-girded their adult ministries. She was known as a Godly mother who daily prayed individually with her 19 children and planted the Word deep within their hearts.

Term: *"Asceticism,"* the erroneous belief that purity and holiness can only be achieved by willful abstinence from bodily pleasure, comforts, and material wealth.

Hymn: "Sweet Hour Of Prayer"
     Lyrics: William Walford c.1840
     Music: William Bradbury c.1861

Sweet hour of prayer, sweet hour of prayer,
that calls me from a world of care
and bids me at my Father's throne,
make all my wants and wishes known.
In seasons of distress and grief,
My soul has often found relief,
and often escaped the tempter's snare,
by thy return, sweet hour of prayer.

Priesthood of the Believer

Focus verse:

S eeing then that we have a great High Priest who has passed through the heavens, Jesus the Son of God, let us hold fast our confession. For we do not have a High Priest who cannot sympathize with our weaknesses, but was in all points tempted as we are, yet without sin. Let us therefore come boldly to the throne of Grace, that we may obtain mercy and find grace to help in time of need.

-Hebrews 4:14-16

Greek: *Hierateuma* (hee-er-at-yoo-mah) priesthood, body of priests, the church.

Theological Note:

Christians have direct access to the Throne of God through the Mediator Jesus Christ our only High Priest, and can respond to His direction and blessing through the Holy Spirit and the Word. All Christians have the ability to minister to one another and to the world as a holy priesthood (I Peter 2:5). Christ calls all believers to share in His priestly duties on earth.

Pastoral Quote:

"Bear up the hands that hang down, by faith and prayer: support the tottering knees. Have you any days of fasting and prayer? Storm the throne of grace and persevere therein, and mercy will come down."

-John Wesley

Reference Verses:

But you are a chosen generation, a royal priesthood, a Holy nation, His own special people, that you may proclaim the praises of Him who called you out of darkness into His marvelous Light.

-I Peter 2:9

And He (Jesus) came and preached peace to you who were afar off and to those who were near. For through Him we both have access by one Spirit to the Father.

-Ephesians 2:17-18

I Peter 2:4-5   I Timothy 2:5   Ephesians 2:14
Romans 12:1

Quote:

"If God sees that my spiritual life will be furthered by giving the things for which I ask, then He will give them, but that is not the end of prayer. The end of prayer is that I come to know God Himself."

-Oswald Chambers
Scottish minister, author
(1874-1917)

Commentary:

The Priesthood of the believer is a vital doctrine of the Christian Faith. Through His redemptive work on the cross, Jesus tore down the wall that separated us from God (Eph.2:14-16). Jesus is our High Priest. We do not need to go through human priests or religious leaders to obtain access to the Father. Jesus is the only Mediator we need. In the book of Hebrews we see the role of Christ and His Priestly duty bestowed by God.

The veil in the Temple separated the *holy of holies* (an area that only the earthly high priest could enter) from all other areas of the Temple grounds. That veil was torn from the top to the bottom at the exact moment of Jesus' death on the cross, declaring that God Himself supplied the sacrifice of the Lamb, and Jesus' blood was sufficient to reconcile man to a holy God (Matt. 27:51). Now those who place their faith in Christ have complete access to the Throne of God.

The Bible says in I Peter chapter 2 that believers are a *royal priesthood* and a *holy priesthood*. This is a profound honor and means that Christians are ordained to carry out the priestly duties of Christ on earth. We are now capable of interceding for one another in prayer, praying directly to God, confessing our sins to one another, bearing one another's burdens, and leading people to Christ and His salvation. We are a living sacrifice and our duty is to serve the Lord and fulfill His purposes on earth (Rom. 12:1).

The priesthood of the believer is an awesome responsibility and privilege. To actually be reconciled to God and approach Him cloaked in the righteousness of Jesus is amazing. This was made possible by *"the Lamb slain from the foundation of the world,"* Jesus, our High Priest and Savior.

"Therefore, in all things He had to be made like His brethren, that He might be a merciful and faithful High

Priest in things pertaining to God, to make propitiation for the sins of the people..."

-Hebrews 2:17

Historical Figure: *Blaise Pascal*

Pascal was born on June 19, 1623. He was a brilliant French mathematician, physicist, and religious philosopher. He was a child prodigy, educated by his father. Later in life, he became a devout Christian and devoted himself to philosophy and theology. Pascal's influence within these academic disciplines are still evident today. He had poor health throughout his life and died two months after his 39th birthday in 1662.

Term: *"Legalism,"* the belief that a person can be saved by trusting in their own good works, efforts, and rituals if they uphold the Old Testament Law. Also a term used for those who strictly adhere to a works type faith and look down on those who do not.

Hymn: *"What a Friend We Have in Jesus"*
Words: Joseph Scriven, 1855
Music: Charles C. Converse, 1868

What a friend we have in Jesus,
all our sins and grief's to bear!
what a privilege to carry
everything to God in prayer!
Oh, what peace we often forfeit,
oh, what needless pain we bear,
all because we do not carry
everything to God in prayer!

Propitiation

Focus Verse:

F or all have sinned and fall short of the glory of God, being justified freely by His grace through redemption that is in Christ Jesus, whom God set forth as a propitiation by His blood.

-Romans 3:23-25a

Greek: *Hilasterion* (hil-as-tay-ree-on) a reconciliation of two parties, to atone for; the covering, the lid of the ark, the mercy seat.

Theological note:

The primary Christian doctrine found here is the blood atonement of Jesus Christ. He has, through His shed blood, restored the broken relationship between God and man that resulted from the Fall. Christ redeemed us by means of a ransom. His death was the price that freed us from guilt and enslavement to sin and the death that sin always produces. In Christ's death God's anger towards our sin was appeased. Jesus took the wrath of God that was meant for us, and as our substitute He placed it upon Himself.

Pastoral Quote:

"Justifying faith implies, not only a divine evidence or conviction that 'God was in Christ, reconciling the world unto Himself,' but sure trust and confidence that Christ died for my sins, that He loved me and gave Himself for me."

-John Wesley
British Anglican minister,
theologian (1703-1791)

Reference verses:

If anyone sins, we have an advocate with the Father, Jesus Christ the righteous and He Himself is the propitiation for our sins, not for ours only but also for the whole world.

-I John 2:1b-2

Therefore, in all things He had to be a merciful and faithful High Priest in things pertaining to God, to make propitiation for the sins of the people.

-Hebrews 2:17

Ephesians 1:7   Hebrews 9:22   Hebrews 9: 23-28
John 3:36

Quote:

"It is a great consolation for me to remember that the Lord, to whom I had drawn near in humble and child-like faith, has suffered and died for me, and that He will look on me in love and compassion."

-Wolfgang Amadeus Mozart
Composer (1756-1791)

Commentary:

In the Old Testament sacrificial system the High Priest would sprinkle the blood of the sacrificial lamb on the *mercy seat* which sat on top of the Ark of the Covenant. This was a plea for the forgiveness of sin for the nation of Israel on the *Day of Atonement*. It was also a fore shadow of the coming final sacrifice by Jesus Christ, the perfect sacrificial Lamb of God, who would be crucified on the cross for all humanity's sin. Only this act of supreme sacrifice and shedding of Jesus' blood could restore the broken relationship between God and man. Now man could be reconciled to a Holy God, and salvation was available to all who would come through the blood of Christ. This supreme atonement by Jesus never had to be repeated.

The atoning sacrifice of Jesus Christ satisfies the demands of God's holy law *and* demonstrates His tremendous grace and love for us. It is important to see that God did not wait for man to somehow appease His wrath against our sin. Where human ritual fell short, God provided the remedy for our hopelessness. He gave His Son who willingly laid down His life at Calvary. In doing so Jesus became the *propitiation* for our sin, our Mercy Seat, and wipes away the record of our transgressions for all that trust in Him. At that very moment on the cross when Jesus cried out, *"It is finished!"* our ransom was *paid in full*. Now those who would place their faith in Jesus Christ would have their sin debt cancelled by the blood of the Son of God.

What should be our response to this ultimate sacrifice and freedom? Gratefulness! People seem to have a hard time believing that there is only one way to God. They get angry about the truth claim of Jesus plainly stating that He is the *only way* to the Father (John 14:6). He could make that exclusive statement because He alone was the propitiation for our sin. Only Jesus could reconcile us to the Father through His profound sacrifice and atonement. In reality, we should be forever astounded that there is even *one* way to Heaven when we realize how utterly corrupted and devastated by sin mankind has been since the Fall.

In view of God's mercy we should strive to lead lives that are honoring to Christ. We must be witnesses of the Father's awesome redemptive love for humanity through His Son. Do not be lulled into thinking this atoning act of Christ was simple and of little consequence. Praise Him daily for His mighty provision that literally pulled you and I out of darkness and placed us into His marvelous light and salvation!

Historical Figure: *David Livingstone*

David Livingstone was born in Scotland at Blantyre, on the Clyde, March 19, 1813. He was born of an impoverished home, but still was able to attend school until the age of 10 when he began working in a cotton mill. By age 12, Livingstone was already interested in the deeper meaning of life, but not until he was 20 did he have a true conversion to Christianity that brought him to the reality of his duty to God. His first time in the pulpit he forgot his whole sermon, and said, *"Friends, I have forgotten all I had to say,"* and ran out of the chapel. He received his medical and theological degrees and prepared to go to Africa where He eventually established a powerful ministry. While traveling in India he learned of the deaths of his son and mother and wrote a book called, *"Fear God and Work Hard,"* that was born out of this difficult time in his life. He went back to Africa and ministered where no missionary had ever gone. He died in Africa on April 29, 1873 while kneeling at his bedside in prayer. His companions brought him back to England to be buried in the Abbey under the Great Slab which says, *"Other sheep I have which are not of this fold: Them also I must bring, and they shall hear my voice."* Livingstone's life example has challenged many Christians to embrace a holy lifestyle and heed the call of missions for their lives.

Term: *"Plenary,"* the whole, complete, entire. Example: *The plenary inspiration of the Bible is a historic Christian doctrine.*

Hymn: *"Nothing But The Blood"*
　　　Words and music: Robert Lowry, 1876

What can wash away my sin?
　Nothing but the blood of Jesus.
What can make me whole again?
　Nothing but the blood of Jesus.
Oh! Precious is the flow that
　makes me white as snow.
No other fount I know, nothing
　but the blood of Jesus.

Regeneration

Focus verse:

B *ut when the kindness and the love of God our Savior toward man appeared, not by works of righteousness which we have done, but according to His mercy He saved us, through the washing of regeneration and renewing of the Holy Spirit, whom He poured out on us abundantly through Jesus Christ our Savior, that having been justified by His grace we should become heirs according to the hope of eternal life.*

-Titus 3:4-7

Greek: *Paliggenesia* (pal-ing-ghen-es-ee'-ah) regeneration, spiritual rebirth, Messianic restoration

Theological note:

Regeneration is a change of heart, wrought by the Holy Spirit, who quickeneth the dead in trespasses and sins enlightening their minds spiritually and savingly to understand the Word of God, and renewing their whole nature, so that they love and practice holiness. It is a work of God's free and special grace alone.

-Southern Baptist Theological Seminary, 1858

Pastoral Quote:

"To fashion a world has less difficulty in it than to create a new life in an ungodly man. For in the creation of the world there was nothing in the way of God: But in the creation of a new heart, there is the old nature opposing the Spirit."

-C.H. Spurgeon

Reference verses:

But as many received Him, to them He gave the right to become children of God, to those who believe in His name: who were born, not of blood, nor of the will of the flesh, nor of the will of man, but of God.

-John 1:12-13

Since you have purified your souls in opening the truth through the Spirit in sincere love of the brethren, love one another fervently with a pure heart, having been born again, not of corruptible seed but incorruptible, through the Word of God which lives and abides forever.

-I Peter 1:22-23

II Corinthians 5:17   I Peter 2:2   Romans 3:10-23
Ephesians 4:17-32

Quote:

"God became man to turn creatures into sons; not simply to produce better men of the old kind but to produce a new kind of man."

-C.S. Lewis

Commentary:

Regeneration is an act of God that brings about the *new birth*. It is the immediate renewal of the human heart, being spiritually dead, now being made alive. This regeneration is possible only through the grace of God and the power of the Holy Spirit. It is necessary because of the fallen state of humanity, and the curse of sin all men have inherited from Adam. Left on our own we would pervert the commands of God and would never seek salvation. Regeneration is the profound and complete spiritual change that is accomplished when Jesus Christ enters the heart of a believer.

Because of our sin Jesus said *"You must be born again"* (John 3:7). Regeneration takes place when the Holy Spirit convicts a person of their sin through the hearing of the Gospel and then believing, receives Christ as their Savior. This regenerative act happens at the moment of conversion and cannot be revoked. It is the radical transformation from being lost in our sin to now being free in Christ, walking in holiness and righteousness. In that amazing moment we are born again. This spiritual act and how it changes the heart and mind of a believer is what baptism symbolizes: once dead in our sin, now raised to new life in Jesus Christ.

This renewal of the heart allows us to love God and seek His will for our lives. We have now begun a new life in Christ, putting off the old, dead life and becoming a new creation in Jesus. In Ephesians chapter 4, Paul shows the dramatic change that becomes evident in the lives of those who are saved. Christians now have victory over sin, no longer slaves to spiritual corruption, because of the regenerative power of the Holy Spirit living within us.

"Therefore if anyone is in Christ, he is a new creation; old things have passed away; behold all things have become new."

-II Corinthians 5:17

Historical Figure: *John Calvin*

Calvin was born on July 10, 1509 in Noyan, France. He was a prominent French theologian and pastor during the Protestant Reformation. He was a principle figure in the development of the system of Christian theology later called *Calvinism*. A controversial religious figure, he broke from the Roman Catholic Church in the 1520's and was forced to flee to Switzerland where he wrote the first edition of *Institutes of the Christian Religion*. His theological writings helped form the Puritan's theology. Calvin himself was influenced greatly by the writings of Augustine. He died in 1564.

Term: *"Cult,"* a religious group that follows a heretical theological system. Usually led by a supposed enlightened leader(s) who becomes the group's authority and undermines, perverts, or dismisses the Holy Bible, claiming "special" knowledge or insight. Their doctrines are opposed to the accepted, established doctrines of the Christian Faith.

Hymn: *"There Is Power In The Blood"*
Words and music: Lewis E. Jones, 1899

Would you be free from the burden of sin?
There's power in the blood, power in the blood;
would you o'er evil a victory win?
There's power in the blood...
There is power, power, wonder working power
in the blood of the Lamb. There is power, power
wonder working power, in the precious blood
of the Lamb.

Repentance

Focus verse:

*F**rom that time Jesus began to preach and to say, "Repent, for the Kingdom of Heaven is at hand."*

-Matthew 4:17

<u>Greek</u>: *Metanoeo* (met-an-o-eh'-o) to change one's mind, direction, or purpose; to think differently

Theological note:

Repentance is an evangelical grace, wherein a person being by the Holy Spirit, made aware of the tremendous evil of his sin, humbles himself before God and with Godly sorrow, detesting his sin and his selfishness, with a purpose and endeavor to walk with God so as to please Him in all things. It is to change one's mind and begin to live differently. To change direction and walk another way.

Pastoral Quote:

"When wicked and unprincipled persons have gone on in a course of sin to the degree that they can scarcely hope for pardon and find that they have reason to fear the just judgment of God for their sins, they begin at first to wish

that there were no God to punish them, which they think would be in their best interests. And so, by degrees, they come to persuade themselves that there is no God. Then they determine to find arguments to back their opinion in order to prove what they are willing to believe."

-John Bunyan
English pastor, author of
The Pilgrim's Progress
(1628-1688)

Reference verses:

Then Peter said to them, " Repent, and let everyone of you be baptized in the name of Jesus Christ for the remission of sins; and you shall receive the gift of the Holy Spirit."
-Acts 2:38

The Lord is not slack concerning His promise, as some count slackness, but is longsuffering towards us, not willing that any should perish but that all should come to repentance.
-II Peter 3:9

Psalm 51   II Corinthians 7:10   II Timothy 2:24-26

Quote:

"Those who wait to repent at the eleventh hour often die at ten-thirty."
-Unknown

Commentary:

Martin Luther used the Latin phrase *"Quorum Deo"* to remind himself and the Reformers that every part of their lives were *"before the face of God."* I believe this is a profound way to approach our lives as Christians today. We must be aware that we are ever before the loving gaze of our Heavenly Father. When we fall, when we sin and break the heart of God, we must bring before Him our repentant heart. I John 1:9 clearly states that when we sin and genuinely confess that sin, Christ is faithful to forgive.

In Psalm 51, King David shares the path of Godly sorrow and repentance. *"For I acknowledge my transgressions, and my sin is always before me. Against You and You only, have I sinned...create in me a clean heart O God."*

Confession, repentance, forgiveness, restoration. To truly repent means we have a change of mind. I now agree with God in regards to my sinfulness. I now seek forgiveness and change the direction I was walking to now walk with Christ. We repent *not* because we are uncomfortable with the feelings and effects of our sin. We repent because we have wronged God. We repent because our sin is an affront to Him.

I am a sinner, Jesus is the Savior. I confess my sin and He, knowing the true motive of my heart, washes me clean. That is an amazing truth. Repentance is a beautiful thing. Do not ever be afraid to approach the Lord when you are weighed down and bound by your sin. As Christians we still certainly sin at times. Often we grow numb and by degrees we slip into sinful behavior and begin to justify our unfaithfulness.

Many believers will stay in that sinful place because of rebellion and stubbornness, but more often they stay there because of deeply felt guilt. Guilt is good for only one thing...to get us to the Cross. Lay down your sin and shame and let Jesus bring forth abundant life. There is no sin greater than the blood of Jesus. It is never too late to begin doing the right thing. Go to Him, trust Him. He has you covered.

The Ten Commandments were given by God to reveal His standard of righteousness to humanity. As we read these standards we are all painfully aware that we fall short of His righteousness and glory (Rom.3:23). These commandments were given so that we would be broken upon them. Through our brokenness we will see our need for a Redeemer. Our genuine awareness of our sin and hopelessness to live up to the standards of God will then cause us to repent of our sin, to feel remorse for our falleness, and look to the Redeemer, our Savior and Lord, Jesus Christ. He alone who spilled His blood on Calvary purchased our redemption and forgiveness of sin. All we must do is repent of our sin, and in faith, believing that He, the Son of God, justifies us and reconciles us to the Father.

Often people will say that telling unbelievers they are sinners in need of repentance is somehow unloving, judgmental, and harsh. They will say, "We should preach a message of love, not scare them with judgment." But we must understand that at the very heart of the message to repent *is* love. Jesus is God, God is love. Everywhere Jesus preached in His earthly ministry He proclaimed foremost the need to repent of sin and follow Him, the Bread of Life (John 6:35). Jesus loved people enough to tell them the truth, and without repentance of sin and believing the Gospel, they would perish and forever be separated from God in Hell. Today we must carry this message to our generation without compromise. Repentance is a primary, vital step towards eternal life in Christ. That is why the message of repentance is ultimately loving and freeing.

If you have not received Jesus as Savior, repentance is the first step toward placing your faith in Him and beginning a new life as a Christian. As the Holy Spirit convicts you of your sin, confess your need for the Savior, and believing on Christ put your faith in Him alone and God will forgive all your sin... past, present, and future. Jesus saves us completely.

Repentance is always surrounded by God's love and grace as He draws us near. Jesus loves you more than you can imagine and desires that you live unchained, blessed, and in spiritual freedom knowing that your ultimate destination is an eternity in Heaven.

Historical Figure: *William Carey*

William Carey was born in Northamptonshire, England on August 17, 1761 and died on June 9, 1834. He was an English Protestant missionary and Baptist minister, known as "the Father of Modern Missions." He was one of the founders of the modern Baptist Missionary Society. He was a missionary in India and he translated the Bible into their languages so they could read it for themselves. Carey has four colleges named after him. Carey's impact on missions cannot be stressed enough. He personally suffered great loss as he took the Gospel across the sea. His perseverance in the Faith is remarkable and his life is a monument to the power of a surrendered life to God.

Term: *"Exegesis,"* The critical interpretation of Scripture. Interpreting the text based solely on what it says in context with surrounding passages and the entirety of Holy Scripture.

Hymn: *"Jesus Paid It All"*
> Words: Elvina M. Hall, 1865
> Music: *"All To Christ,"* John T. Grape, 1868

I hear the Savior say,
Thy strength indeed is small,
child of weakness, watch and pray,
find in Me thine all in all.
Jesus paid it all, all to Him I owe;
Sin had left a crimson stain,
He washed it white as snow.

The Resurrection of
Jesus Christ

Focus verse:

*J esus said unto her, "I am the resurrection and the life,
he who believes in Me, though he may die, he shall
live."*

-John 11:25

Greek: *Anastasis* (an-as'-tas-is) to stand again, resurrection
from death

Theological Note:

The resurrection of Jesus Christ demonstrated His victory over sin, Hell, and the grave. Christianity rests on this historic event. This divine act proved that Jesus was the Son of God and that eternal life could be found only in Christ. This was a bodily resurrection, a renewing of Jesus' body, now glorified and incorruptible. This glorious event guarantees the Christian believer's salvation, justification, and hope of Heaven.

Pastoral Quote:

"We are not preaching the Gospel of a dead Christ, but a living Christ who sits exalted at the Father's right hand, and is living to save all who put their trust in Him. That is why those of us who really know the Gospel never have any crucifixes around our churches or homes. The crucifix represents a dead Christ hanging languid on a cross of shame. But we are not pointing men to a dead Christ; We are preaching a living Christ. He lives exalted at God's right hand and He saves to the uttermost all who come to God by Him."

-Henry Allen (H.A.) Ironside
Canadian born, pastor of
Moody Church, Chicago.
Bible teacher, author
(1876-1951)

Reference verses:

But the angel answered and said to the women, "Do not be afraid, for I know that you seek Jesus who was crucified. He is not here; for He is risen, as He said. Come see the place where the Lord lay. And go quickly and tell His disciples that He is risen from the dead, and indeed He is going before you into Galilee; there you will see Him. Behold, I have told you."
-Matthew 28: 5-7

That I may know Him and the power of His resurrection, and the fellowship of His sufferings, being conformed to His death, if by any means, I may attain to the resurrection from the dead.

-Philippians 3:10-11

Romans 6:5-11   Luke 9:22   Mark 16:1-8
Luke 24:1-7 Hebrews 11:35

Quote:

"The Resurrection is the central theme in every Christian sermon reports in the Book of Acts. The resurrection, and its consequences were the Gospel or 'Good News' which the Christian brought...the miracles of the resurrection and the theology of that miracle comes first. The biography comes later as a comment on it. Nothing could be more unhistorical than to pick out selected sayings of Christ from the Gospels and to regard those as the data and the rest of the New Testament as a construction upon it. The first fact in the history of Christendom is a number of people who say they have seen the resurrection."

C.S. Lewis
British scholar, author
(1898-1963)

Commentary:

The resurrection of Jesus Christ from the dead is a primary Christian doctrine. This event was the turning point in human history. It is this truth that sets Jesus apart from all previous and future religious figures. All other religious leaders have, or will, bow to death and lie in a grave, powerless and defeated. Jesus lives. The resurrection proved that He indeed was the only begotten Son of God and that everything He spoke and preached was the Word of God. Christianity hinges on the certainty of Christ rising from the dead. The New Testament writers of the Gospels proclaimed to the world that Jesus Christ left a tomb standing open wide. They were actual witnesses to the risen Christ, testifying that Jesus lives and He alone is *"the Way, the Truth, and the Life."*

It is a fact that Jesus died by crucifixion two thousand years ago, the sinless Son of God bearing the sins of all humanity. The day that Jesus hung on the cross the world became completely dark between the sixth and ninth hours. An earthquake and all-consuming darkness brought even the bravest Roman soldier trembling to his knees. Jesus described Hell to His disciples as "outer darkness," meaning there is absolutely no light or hope. God brought a glimpse of Hell to Jerusalem in those few hours. Jesus atoned for a world engulfed by sin, paying our penalty of death, suffering crushing pain and unimaginable sorrow for our pardon. Jesus' horrible death purchased our freedom and appeased the wrath of Almighty God, forever penetrating our hopelessness with the brilliant light of salvation.

Later that day Jesus' body was taken off the cross, and as far as the world was concerned He was just another executed criminal to be buried and left to rot and fade into obscurity. But redemption's story was not yet complete. On the third day a stone was rolled away, and a tomb was left empty because the grave could not hold the risen Savior! Jesus, firstborn from the dead, has prepared the only way for us to live eternally. His resurrection from the dead demonstrated His absolute victory over Satan, Hell, and the last enemy, Death.

His resurrection was a *bodily* resurrection. This was not some surreal "spirit" rising from the dead, or as some would believe a symbolic "raising" that alludes to an emotional hope in the "overcoming" human spirit. No, Jesus literally was dead and now He lives. Without the bodily resurrection we have no hope and Christianity is meaningless. Paul states this clearly when he says, *"If Christ is not risen, your faith is futile; you are still in your sins! Then also those who have fallen asleep in Christ have perished. If in this life only we have hope in Christ, we are of all men the most pitiable"* (I Cor.15:17-19). Jesus' resurrection insures *our* bodily resurrection (I Cor. 15:50-57).

Hope is good if it is real. False hope is cruel and pointless. The end result of genuine hope is deliverance and joy. The resurrection of Jesus Christ places in the heart of Christian's real hope. Not only the tremendous hope of eternal life, but hope in this life that when things seem so dark, glorious light can shine, shattering suffocating despair and replacing it with joy. Death is ruined as joyous life shouts the victory, and a shroud is replaced with the royal robe of a King. **Jesus is risen!** You can trust Him with every part of your life. He is the Victor, and in Christ, we as believers, are forever victorious!

<u>Historical Figure:</u> *Peter Cartwright*

Cartwright was born on September 1, 1785 in Amherst County, Virginia. He was an early American *"hellfire and brimstone"* preacher who was also a missionary to Native Americans. His preaching ministry helped fuel the Second Great Awakening. He baptized over 12,000 people throughout his ministry. He was one of the first "horseback riding preachers" who traveled from town to town to minister to those without a full-time pastor. In a campaign for a United States Congress seat in 1846 he lost to Abraham Lincoln. He then settled in Illinois. He died on September 25, 1872.

<u>**Term:**</u> *"Soteriology,"* from two Greek words *"sozo"* (to save) and *"logos"* (meaning, *word*). It is the doctrine of the study of God's work in salvation ("soter," *savior*). How through the death and resurrection of Christ, man's redemption is accomplished.

Hymn: *"Low In The Grave He Lay"*
   Words and music: Robert Lowry, 1874

Low in the grave He lay, Jesus my Savior!
waiting the coming day, Jesus my Lord!
Up from the grave He arose, with a mighty
triumph o'er His foes; He arose the victor
from the dark domain, and He lives forever
with His saints to reign.
He arose, He arose, Hallelujah! Christ arose!

Salvation

Focus verse:

*T**hat if you confess with your mouth the Lord Jesus and believe in your heart that God has raised Him from the dead, you will be saved. For with the heart one believes unto righteousness, and with the mouth confession is made unto salvation.*

-Romans 10: 9-10

Greek: *Soteria* (so-tay-ree-ah) salvation, save, rescue, health, deliverance

Theological note:

The saving of sinful man from the righteous judgment of God. Christ saving us from damnation and eternal separation from God. To be forgiven and cleansed of all sin and reconciled to a Holy God by the blood of Christ and being made a new creation. Salvation is found in Jesus Christ alone and is a free gift from God, accepted by faith, and bestowed upon us by His grace.

Pastoral quote:

"Either sin is with you, lying on your shoulders, or it is lying on Christ, the Lamb of God. Now if it is lying on your back, you are lost. But if it is resting on Christ, you are free and you are saved."

-Martin Luther
German theologian,
pastor (1483-1546)

Reference Verse:

Jesus answered, "Most assuredly I say to you, unless one is born again he cannot enter the Kingdom of God."

-John 3:3

Therefore, if anyone is in Christ, he is a new creation, old things have passed away, behold all things have become new.

-II Corinthians 5:17

For the Son of man has come to seek and to save that which was lost.

-Luke 19:10

Ephesians 2:8-10   I Timothy 2:3-4   Titus 3:4-6
I John 2:1-2

Quote:

"Aim at Heaven and you will get earth thrown in; aim at earth and you get neither."

-C. S. Lewis

Commentary:

The main thrust of the Gospel of Jesus Christ is the salvation of man. The Gospel declares that God will save all those who come to Him through faith in Jesus Christ. The *Gospel*, or *Evangel* (from the Greek *euangelion,* meaning *"good news"*), is the proclamation that Jesus was crucified, buried, and risen from the dead (I Cor. 15:1-4). The Apostle Paul stated, *"I am not ashamed of the Gospel of Christ, for it is the power of God to salvation for everyone who believes..."* (Rom.1:16). Salvation delivers man from the power of sin, the wrath of God, and an eternal Hell.

We must understand that salvation is a *gift* from God. It cannot be earned, bought, or imitated. There is one way to God and that pathway is only through the death and resurrection of Jesus Christ (John 14:6). Our salvation was purchased at an unfathomable cost because the price was the death of the Son of God. We should never underestimate the value of this gift that was so graciously and lovingly bestowed on us by the Father.

Faith comes through the *hearing of the Word* and we are called to declare the Gospel, the way of salvation, to all men (Rom.10:17). The Gospel is a proclamation, not a suggestion or an offer. It is the truth of how one may obtain eternal life and forgiveness of sin. We are not saved by believing in doctrines and creeds, or human standards and rituals. *We are saved by believing in the crucified Christ who has risen from the dead to everlasting life*. Our faith is placed in Him alone for our salvation and hope. When we are saved our name is written in the *Lamb's Book of Life* as an eternal record that we have been purchased by Jesus Christ (Luke 10:20, Rev. 21:27).

In John 5:24 Jesus tells us clearly that we can know we are saved. *"Most assuredly, I say to you, he who hears My word and believes in Him who sent Me has everlasting life, and shall not come into judgment, but has passed from death into life."* Christians do not need to wonder if they are actually saved. Our emotions can bring doubt but our salvation rests on the solid rock of Jesus Christ.

There are no pre-conditions to being saved other than responding to the Gospel under the conviction of the Holy Spirit. This conviction brings forth a desire to repent of our sin and to be reconciled to God. We are then led to place our faith, our belief, in Jesus alone to accomplish the complete forgiveness of our sins, delivering us from unrighteousness, and thus becoming a member of the family of God. The simplicity of the Gospel is why children can receive Christ and have a genuine salvation experience. This *Good News* is for all mankind, and we are to receive Jesus with child-like faith (Mark 10:15).

It is clear Biblically that Christ died for the world, providing salvation to all who would call on His name (John 3:16). To believe that only a few "elect" have the opportunity to be saved and the majority of humanity is damned, is in effect saying that Jesus' atonement is inferior to Adam's sin. God desires that all people would repent and come to Him. He does not want any to perish (II Peter 3:9). His grace is extended to all, but man's freewill cannot be violated. God will not force His gift of salvation upon anyone. God's sovereignty is at the heart of pre-destination. He knew from the foundation of the world who would accept the gift of His Son and those who would reject Christ.

Bible study and teaching are vital for correct doctrine and faith practices, but it is our response to the simplicity of the Gospel that begins our personal, eternal relationship with Jesus Christ. After we are born again we begin to grow in our faith. Through the diligent study of Scripture, along with a developing prayer life, we then mature in our relationship with the Lord.

The greatest miracle is not that someone gets out of a wheelchair and walks, or that a blind man is healed and can now see. The greatest miracle will always be that a sinful, broken, hopelessly lost person responds to the Gospel and is born again, gloriously saved, cleansed and restored by the power of Jesus Christ. That we have passed from death to life by faith in the finished work of Christ is a miraculous reality of the love and sovereignty of God.

So often people contend that there must be many ways to be "saved" and end up in their idea of a heaven, or paradise. The truth is that if God did offer 100 ways to be saved, the hardness of man's heart would have demanded 101. When Jesus declared that He was the only way to the Father, the only way to Heaven, He made a very exclusive statement (John 14:6). Jesus could make that declaration because He is God and He knew resurrection day was coming. He is the *only way* because He alone has conquered death.

That is good news! We are now called to proclaim this amazing, life-changing *Evangel* and urged to take on the responsibility of being *evangelists* in our day to day lives (II Tim. 4:5). We are to be ready to preach the Word and joyfully declare the *Good News* that sin is powerless, death is destroyed, and Hell has been conquered!

We have the privilege as the Church to introduce people to the *One* who first proclaimed the Gospel, our Lord and Savior, Jesus.

"The Spirit of the Lord is upon Me because He has anointed Me to preach the Gospel to the poor, He has sent Me to heal the brokenhearted, To proclaim liberty to the captives and recovery of sight to the blind, to set at liberty those who are oppressed; to proclaim the acceptable year of the Lord."

-Luke 4:18-19

Historical Figure: *Billy Graham*

Billy Graham was born on November 7, 1918 in Charlotte, North Carolina where he still resides. He is an internationally known evangelist of the Southern Baptist denomination. He has been a spiritual adviser to multiple U.S. presidents, ranked in the world as one of the most admired people, as well as being the most trusted modern day preacher. He has preached to more people than any minister that has ever lived and millions of people have accepted Christ through his ministry outreach. He is the founder of the Billy Graham Evangelistic Association (BGEA), Christianity Today magazine, The Cove Christian seminar & retreat center in North Carolina, and the Christian radio station 106.9 WMIT. His son, Franklin Graham, has assumed the leadership of the BGEA.

Term: *"Apologetics,"* to make a defense for the Christian Faith. To defend the Word of God and Scriptural truth claims.

Hymn: *"At The Cross"*
　　　　Words: Isaac Watts, 1707
　　　　Music: Ralph E. Hudson, 1885

Alas, and did my Savior bleed,
and did my Sovereign die?
Would He devote that Sacred Head
for sinners such as I?
At the cross, at the cross
where I first saw the light,
and the burden of my heart
rolled away, it was there by
faith I received my sight,
and now I am happy all the day!

Sanctification

Focus Verse:

F or both He who sanctifies and those who are being sanctified are all of one, for which reason He is not ashamed to call them brethren.

-Hebrews 2:11

<u>Greek</u>: *Hagiazo* (hag-ee-ad'-zo) to make holy, purify or consecrate

Theological note:

The work of God's free grace, whereby we are renewed in the whole man after the image of God, and are enabled more and more to die unto sin, and live unto righteousness.

-Westminster Shorter Catechism

Pastoral quote:

"Be assured, if you walk with Him and look to Him, and expect help from Him, God will never fail you."

-George Mueller
German evangelist,
orphanage founder
(1805-1898)

Reference verses:

For this is the will of God, your sanctification; that you should abstain from sexual immorality; that each of you should know how to possess his own vessel in sanctification.
-I Thessalonians 4:3-4

But of Him you are in Christ Jesus, who became for us wisdom from God; and righteousness and sanctification and redemption.
-I Corinthians 1:30

Philippians 2:12-13   Romans 15:16
I Corinthians 6:11   John 17:17-19

Quote:

"It's not that the Christian Faith has been tried and found difficult, but rather it's been found difficult and left untried."
-Gilbert Keith (G. K.) Chesterton
English writer, philosopher,
journalist (1874-1936)

Commentary:

The word *sanctification* comes from the Latin *santificatio*, meaning to consecrate or to be in the process of becoming holy. Sanctification is always joined with the salvation experience. It is the work of the Holy Spirit that begins to transform us on a spiritual and moral level as we walk with the Lord. This process brings maturity and the desire of holiness into the believer's life.

The word *sanctify* was actually a secular term that meant to use something for its original purpose or designation. For example, a cup was meant to hold water and it was *sanctified* when water was in it. In salvation we are securely redeemed in Jesus, and sanctification is our living out this reality day to day, growing in the grace and knowledge of Christ, being properly used as vessels of the Holy Spirit.

The cross of Jesus has made it possible for us to move from a hopeless, profane existence to one of holiness and acceptance. We are now able to be a part of the Kingdom of God, to become the dwelling place of the Holy Spirit, and to perform good works for God's glory. We are also sanctified to worship God and enter into His presence by the blood of Jesus (Heb. 13:12).

As Christians we are to embrace this sanctification process and live lives that honor Christ. Regeneration is the moment of spiritual birth; Sanctification is the ongoing growth of our faith in Christ. We should desire to grow and become mature, faithful, followers of Jesus. We should also keep in mind that it is God who empowers us to walk in holiness and He will continue to bring us into a right relationship with Him because ultimately this is His will for our lives (Phil. 2:13).

In Ephesians chapter 2, Paul says that we are God's *workmanship*. This action of sanctification is His way of building us into His "masterpiece" for His glory, purpose, and our eternal benefit. Sanctification is putting into practice what we already are in position: *Righteous in Christ*. It matters how we live as Christians. Let your life impact your generation as you strive to walk in the power, holiness and grace of Jesus Christ, being ever aware of His sanctifying work within you.

<u>Historical Figure:</u> *Oswald Chambers*

Chambers was born on July 24, 1874 in Aberdeen, Scotland. He was a prominent early 20th century Scottish Protestant Christian minister and teacher. Chambers is best known as the author of the widely read devotional, *"My*

Utmost for His Highest." He was greatly influenced by Spurgeon. He died in Egypt on November 15, 1917.

Term: *"Antinomianism,"* *"anti"* means *against* and *"nomos"* means the *law*. The unbiblical practice of living without regard of God's righteousness, using grace as a license to sin (Romans 6:12).

Hymn: *My Jesus, I Love Thee*
        Words and music:
        William R. Featherstone, 1842-1878
        Adoniram J. Gordon, 1836-1895

My Jesus, I love Thee, I know Thou art mine,
For Thee all the follies of sin I resign;
My gracious Redeemer, my Saviour art Thou;
If ever I loved Thee, my Jesus, tis' now.

The Second Coming of Christ

Focus verse:

B *ehold, He is coming with clouds, and every eye will see Him, even they who pierced Him. And all tribes of the earth will mourn because of Him. Even so, amen.*

-Revelation 1:7

<u>**Greek**</u>: *Parousia* (par-oo-see'-ah) being near, presence, coming

Theological note:

The physical return of Jesus Christ to earth. At the Second Coming, Jesus will be seen by every person on earth as He descends from Heaven. This event will usher in the Kingdom of God on earth. It is the Second Coming that should produce joy in the heart of all believers and bring a sense of urgency to evangelize and serve the Lord in every generation. The timing of this event is known only by the Father (Matthew 24:36), and is seen by the Church as imminent.

Pastoral quote:

"The immense step from the babe in Bethlehem to the living, reigning triumphant Lord Jesus, returning to earth for His own people...that is the glorious truth proclaimed throughout Scripture. As the bells ring out the joys of Christmas, may we also be alert for the final trumpet that will announce His return, when we shall always be with Him."

-Alan Redpath
British born evangelist,
pastor of Moody Church, Chicago
(1907-1989)

Reference verses:

But the day of the Lord will come as a thief in the night, in which the heavens will pass away with a great noise, and the elements will melt with fervent heat; both the earth and the works that are in it will be burned up.

-II Peter 3:10

Then they will see the Son of Man coming in the clouds with great power and glory.

-Mark 13:26

Mark 13:14-27   I Thessalonians 3:13
Revelation 19:11-16   Acts 1:9-11

Quote:

"The doctrine of the Second Coming of Christ is deeply uncongenial to the whole evolutionary or developmental character of modern thought. We have been taught to think of the world as something that grows slowly towards per-

fection, something that 'progresses' or 'evolves.' Christian apocalyptic offers us no such hope."
-Clive Staples (C.S.) Lewis
British scholar, author
(1898-1963)

Commentary:

Both the Old Testament and the New Testament declare the return of Jesus Christ, the Messiah, to rule over the earth. At His second coming Christ will bring to an end world history as we now understand it. This is a primary doctrine of Christianity. Jesus' return will be personal, physical, triumphant and for the whole world to see.

There are 1,845 Biblical references pertaining to the Second Coming. 318 of these are found in the New Testament. This doctrine is revealed in 17 of the Old Testament books. It is also taught in 7 out of every 10 chapters of the New Testament. Other than the subject of Faith it is the most mentioned teaching in the New Testament.

In the Upper Room before His death on the cross, Jesus told His disciples *"I will come again and receive you to Myself"* (John 14:3). At His return every knee will bow and every tongue will confess that Jesus is Lord (Phil.2:10-11). Wickedness will be crushed and there will be no more human rebellion as Satan is banished. Jesus not only returns as King but also as Judge.

After the Great Tribulation period Christ will set up His earthly reign from Jerusalem and govern God's Kingdom with His saints. His second coming will begin what is known as the *Millennial Reign of Christ*. This is a period of one thousand years of peace, abundance, and sole worship of God.

Many people have the false assumption that humanity will evolve and progress into societies of unity, trust, abundance, and perfection. This humanistic dream of man becoming peaceful and good on his own is a hopeless utopian fairytale. The human heart is wicked and will never be able to live without lust, war, murder, and greed (Jeremiah 17:9). The only true hope of mankind is for those who place their faith in Christ and His coming kingdom.

Jesus' earthly miracles attested to what would one day be a reality for all believers when the curse of sin no longer holds sway over mankind and creation. In the Millennium people will not be bound by, or suffer from, hunger, blindness, sickness, deafness, decay and death. The Second Coming will usher in a glorious age of amazing abundance and life everlasting with Jesus the focus of our praise and worship.

In Revelation chapter 5 the Apostle John gets a glimpse of this coming reality when he declares, *"And every creature which is in heaven and on the earth and under the earth and such as are in the sea, and all that are in them, I heard saying, 'Blessing and honor and glory and power be to Him who sits on the Throne, and to the Lamb, forever, and ever!'"*

The time of Christ's coming is known only by the Father and we are to not set dates (Matt. 24:36). But we are to be on the alert in every generation as if He were coming today (Matt. 24:42). We should be careful to proclaim the Gospel and urgently call people to repentance. In the last days Jesus said scoffers would be plentiful and ridicule the idea of His return to earth saying, *"Where is the promise of His coming?"* (II Peter 3:3-4). But we as believers should always let the promise of His return encourage and motivate us to live for Jesus Christ, urgently reaching out to those who are still in darkness.

Bible scholars reveal that there are many more prophecies of Jesus' second coming than those of His first coming. The absolute fact is that Jesus Christ will return and there is no power on earth that can stop Him. John again says, *"We know that when He (Jesus) is revealed, we shall be like Him, for we shall see Him as He is. And everyone who has this hope in Him purifies himself, just as He is pure"* (I John 3:2-3).

God's promises are sure. Jesus is coming back. What an awesome truth, what an awesome God we serve!

"...Men of Galilee, why do you stand gazing into heaven? This same Jesus, who was taken up from you into Heaven, will so come in like manner as you saw Him go into Heaven."

-Acts 1: 11

Historical Figure: *Dietrich Bonhoeffer*

Dietrich Bonhoeffer (1906-1945) was a German pastor, theologian, participant in the German Resistance Movement against Nazism, and a founding member of the Confessing Church. He was greatly influenced by the theologian Karl Barth whom he had a personal friendship with. During WWII He became an outspoken opponent to Hitler and the horror of the holocaust and was banned from preaching and teaching. He was arrested, imprisoned, and brutally hanged just weeks before the war ended. He once said, *"One act of obedience is better than one hundred sermons."*

Term: *"Existentialism,"* Philosophical viewpoint that emphasizes human freewill and abilities. Subjectivity and individual choice are elevated above moral and spiritual absolutes.

Hymn: *"Joy To The World"*
        Music: George Frederick Handel
        Arranged, Lowell Mason, 1839
        Words: Isaac Watts, 1719

Joy to the world! The Lord has come,
let earth receive her King; let every heart
prepare Him room, and Heaven and nature sing,
and Heaven and nature sing, and Heaven, and
Heaven and nature sing!

*(Isaac Watts actually wrote this song about the Second Coming of Christ, not His birth.)

Servanthood

Focus verse:

*J*ust as the Son of Man did not come to be served, but to serve, and to give His life a ransom for many.

-Matthew 20:28

Greek: *Diakoneo* (dee-ak-on-eh'-o) to wait upon, to serve, deacon

Theological note:

Servanthood is the state or condition of one who lives as a servant. A servant is under submission to another person or persons. For Christians, this means submission to Christ first, and then submission to one another. To willingly minister to others rather than living for self. To put other's needs before our own, using Christ as our example.

Pastoral Quote:

"Every man must serve somebody: we have no choice as to that fact. Those who have no masters are slaves to themselves. Depend upon it, you will either serve Satan or Christ, either self or the Savior."

-C.H. Spurgeon

"There is only one relationship that matters, and that is your personal relationship to a personal Redeemer and Lord. Let everything else go, but maintain that at all costs, and God will fulfill His purpose through your life. One individual life may be of priceless value to God's purposes, and yours may be that life."

-Oswald Chambers

Reference Verses:

No one can serve two masters: for either he will hate the one and love the other, or else he will be loyal to the one and despise the other. You cannot serve God and mammon.

-Matthew 6:24

I beseech you therefore, brethren, by the mercies of God, that you present your bodies a living sacrifice, holy, acceptable to God which is your reasonable service.

-Romans 12:1

John 12:26 John 15:20 Galatians 5:13 Hebrews 9:14

Quote:

"We make a living by what we get; we make a life by what we give."

-Sir Winston Churchill
British Prime Minister
writer, artist (1874-1965)

Commentary:

Spurgeon once said that, *"A Jesus who never wept could never wipe away my tears."* Jesus is our model of servanthood for He was the *Suffering Servant* leading His Church into a lifestyle of ministry and care for others. We too are called to weep with the afflicted, care for the lost, and bring comfort to the oppressed. This characteristic of the Christian life becomes more evident as we mature in Christ.

Leaders of the church should always first be marked as servants before they take an authoritative position in a fellowship. For example, deacons are first and foremost servants of the local body. They are to make sure the ministers of the congregation have ample time for prayer and study of the Word. They are not in that position to dictate or guide the preaching ministry of the Church. Pastors should also have a servant's heart and desire to be a compassionate undershepherd to their people.

If we are to grow and mature into the likeness of Jesus Christ we must experience giving ourselves in ministry and to others (Phil. 1:4). We live in a day where most people are concerned primarily with their own happiness and comfort. As Christians we must stand against the pull toward selfishness and realize our greatest gift to others is one of lowliness and humility. We are called to put other people's needs before our own needs and desires. The real heart of Christianity is loving Jesus, serving Him, obeying His Word, and loving God's people. Out of this profound relationship with Jesus we are then empowered to be servants filled with the Holy Spirit. We serve Jesus because He first humbled Himself for our eternal benefit.

We must be careful to serve God and others with righteous motives. We should fight the temptation to only do something good for someone because in the end we will receive the praise of men. This is hypocritical and will yield no fruit. We must understand the sacrificial nature of being a true servant (Rom. 12:1-2). Not only is sacrifice often involved, we are to also be fully surrendered to God's will. As we yield to the Holy Spirit we become effective in serving others (Eph. 5:18). We must yield our will to the Holy Spirit seeking God's power to be displayed in our weakness and frailty.

The closer you walk with Christ the more you will purely desire to serve those around you with a heart of thankfulness and mercy.

Jesus' example reveals His plan for the Church to greatly impact the world and be a blessing to all people. It is the love of Christ that bids people to come to Him. Servanthood displays His amazing love to the world through ordinary people like you and me who serve an extraordinary Savior. We are Jesus' hands and feet, willing to lovingly serve and put other people's needs before our own.

Historical Figure: *James Gilmour*

James Gilmour, born in 1843, was a Scottish missionary to Mongolia. He was a devout Christian who lived out a very strict but compassionate Faith. He was led to bring the Gospel and serve people immersed in Buddhism. Often times he felt profound loneliness and isolation as he labored to win converts to Christ. He traveled by foot, often times mistaken for a tramp because of his clothing and appearance. He mostly slept in a tent as he traveled along with the nomadic people of eastern Mongolia. He used medicine, healing, and music to open doors to minister to the Mongolian people. Gilmour married his wife, Emily, in 1874 and she became a great help and companion in the ministry. They had three children. She died in 1885. James died six years later in 1891 from typhus at the age of 47. He influenced many to follow the call of the Lord and go to the farthest points of the world to preach the Gospel.

Term: *"Typology,"* a method of interpreting some parts of Scripture by seeing a pattern elsewhere in Scripture. A "type" is a representation of one thing of another.
Example: Adam was a *type* of Christ. (Romans 5:14)

Hymn: *"When We Walk With The Lord"*
    Words: John H. Sammis, 1887
    Music: *"Trust and Obey,"* Daniel B. Towner, 1887

When we walk with the Lord in the light of His Word,
What a glory He sheds on our way! Let us do His good will,
He abides with us still, and with all who will trust and obey.
Trust and obey, for there's no other way, to be happy in
Jesus, but to trust and obey.

Sexual Immorality

Focus verse:

F or this is the will of God, your sanctification: that you should abstain from sexual immorality.

-I Thessalonians 4:3

Greek: *Porneia* (por-ni-ah) fornication, harlotry, adultery, incest

Theological note:

All sexual relations outside of the bonds of marriage are acts of fornication and deemed unclean and sinful by God. Sexual immorality includes pre-marital sex, adultery, molestation, rape, pornography, homosexuality, prostitution, and incest. Sexual sin always brings a devaluing to human life and perverts the sanctity of marriage.

Pastoral quote:

"Surely the very holiness of God that puts in us a desire to be holy is a guarantee to us that He will help us to be holy. He that makes us long for purity will work it in us."

-C.H. Spurgeon

Reference verses:

Do you not know that your bodies are members of Christ? Shall I then take the members of Christ and make them members of a harlot? Certainly not! Or do you not know that he who is joined to a harlot is one body with her?

-I Corinthians 6:15-16

Flee sexual immorality. Every sin a man does is outside the body, but he that commits sexual immorality sins against his own body. Or do you not know that your body is the temple of the Holy Spirit who is in you, whom you have from God, and you are not your own? For you were bought at a price; therefore glorify God in your body and in your Spirit, which are God's.

-I Corinthians 6:18-20

Hebrews 2:18   I Corinthians 6:13   Hebrews 13:4
I Corinthians 10:13

Quote:

"Do not say that you have a chaste mind if your eyes are unchaste, because an unchaste eye betrays an unchaste heart."

-Saint Augustine

Commentary:

The Bible condemns all sexual sin and repeatedly warns against this particular sinful behavior. The reason is seen in Paul's writing to the Corinthian church when he says, **"Flee sexual immorality, every sin that a man does is outside the body, but he who commits sexual immorality sins against his own body."** All sin is detestable to God but fornication takes us into a spiritual realm that other types of sin do not.

Any sexual union outside of the bonds of marriage plunge us into spiritual, emotional, and physical destruction. The consequences are harsh, far-reaching, and can last a lifetime.

Human sexuality can be a beautiful experience in the context of marriage but outside of marriage it makes us slaves to sin and can never bring glory to God or honor to our lives. We often follow the wrong path with our sexuality when we refuse to trust God's Word. His Word and Spirit sets us free, all Satan can do is corrupt and enslave. We must daily make a deliberate choice to follow Christ and seek truth in every aspect of our lives. We as Christians are called to walk differently than the world around us that is swept up in lust and fornication which results from their blindness towards God (Eph. 4:17-18 and I John 2:16).

Sexual temptation and addiction is prevalent in our society and as Christians we must learn to be self-controlled and sensitive to the Holy Spirit's leading. You need to understand how valuable you are to God, and that fornication always brings a devaluing to your life. Sexual purity is attainable and begins with our thought life. Satan will always attack our minds first. *Temptation is not sin.* We often live with false guilt because we are tempted to sin. *Giving into the temptation is the sin.* For example, you may be tempted to watch pornography but you do not because you stand against that temptation and refuse to justify that behavior. God is pleased with the stand you have made.

We must be careful what we put before our eyes, the places we walk into, and how we deal with day to day relationships. We must have boundaries that we will not cross, being aware of our tendency to take things further than we should. It is interesting that in the case of satanic oppression we are to resist, but when confronted with sexual immorality we are to run away. This should give us some idea how deep the consequences of fornication really are. Above all, sexual sin is against God and grieves the Holy Spirit who lives within us.

God designed us to enjoy sex and physical intimacy within the marriage covenant. He has placed a prohibition against pre-marital and adulterous sex because He knows the destructive nature of this behavior and the betrayal against Him and the institution of the family. In the case of adultery, Christians will often try to justify an affair. When we do this we are saying to God that we find value in our lustful behavior. God will never go against His holy nature. He will never bless sin no matter how we try to twist His Word or manipulate those around us.

The fallout of adulterous affairs has left us with fractured families producing angry, fragile, displaced children and adults. As the Church we must live up to a higher standard and take seriously our responsibilities to live pure and holy lives before God (Rom. 12:1-2). In doing so, we help protect our families and fellowships, providing a safe place for young people to flourish instead of being victimized.

When fighting sexual temptation we need to learn to stand against temptation (James 4:7), repent of our sin to God and seek forgiveness (I John 1:9), confess sin and seek counsel from a mature brother or sister in Christ (James 5:16), turn your attention to Godly pursuits and His praise (Heb. 13:14), hide God's Word deep in your heart (Psalm 119:11 and Heb. 4:12), and seek His grace and strength when you are weak (II Cor. 12:9).

This temptation to sin sexually can be a tough battle but it does not have to be one that keeps you defeated, and powerless. You may have fallen in this area and continue to struggle. Please know that Jesus will forgive you no matter what you have done. His forgiveness is deep, real, and complete, and *He is the God who makes all things new*. Run to Him, not away from Him. You can be victorious in this area of your life, and your purity is well worth the fight. It is certainly worth surrendering all to God.

Ultimately we are to bring our thought life under the obedience of Christ. How? We must purposely turn from sinful images, fantasies, and inappropriate relationships. We then set our minds on better, holy things (Phil. 4:8). In Proverbs 25:28 we are given this warning: *"Whoever has no rule over his own spirit is like a city broken down, without walls."* Ancient cities that had unguarded and inferior walls were constantly vulnerable to enemy attacks. To keep the enemy of our soul from conquering us in this area of our lives we must engage our will, being self-controlled, guarding our hearts and not being led by our emotions and lust...ultimately yielding to the Holy Spirit within us.

For the weapons of our warfare are not carnal (fleshly) but mighty in God for pulling down strongholds, casting down arguments and every high thing that exalts itself against the knowledge of God, bringing every thought into captivity to the obedience of Christ, and being ready to punish all disobedience when your obedience is fulfilled.

-II Corinthians 10:4-6

Historical Figure: *Malcolm Muggeridge*

Muggeridge was born in Croydon, England on March 24, 1903. He was a British journalist, author, media personality, and soldier-spy. He worked in the British secret intelligence agency and also was a writer during World War II. He professed to be an agnostic most of his life, but later converted to Christianity. He wrote books testifying to how Christ had utterly transformed his life. Muggeridge has had a strong influence on evangelical Christian apologists and writers. He died May 29, 1990.

Term: *"Hedonism,"* the destructive idea that pleasure is the principle good and proper goal of all human action. To indulge in selfish behavior.

Hymn: *"I Surrender All"*
     Words: Judson W. Van Deventer, 1896
     Music: Winfield S. Weeden, 1896

All to Jesus I surrender, all to Him I freely give;
I will ever love and trust Him, in His presence
daily live.
I surrender all, I surrender all
All to Thee my precious Savior, I surrender all.

Sin and the Fall of Man

F or all have sinned and fall short of the glory of God.
                                                    -Romans 3:23

Greek: *Hamartia* (ham-ar-tee'-ah) sin, an offense, missing the mark

Theological note:

When Adam and Eve disobeyed God's command in the Garden of Eden to not eat of the Tree of the Knowledge of Good and Evil, sin entered creation and the heart of Man. Adam, representing all of mankind, brought death upon creation that in its original state was perfect. Sin is anything that is contrary to the law and will of God. Sin is lawlessness that leads to death and separation from God. All humans are under the penalty of sin and are dead in their sin and unrighteousness. They are made alive only in Jesus Christ, placing their faith and trust in Him as Lord and Savior, thus securing the forgiveness of all sin, being made righteous before God, and having eternal life.

Pastoral Quote:

"In nothing is the corrupt memory of man more treacherous than in this, that it is apt to forget God; because out of sight, He is out of mind; and here begins all the wickedness that is in the world; they have perverted their way, for they have forgotten the Lord their God."

-Matthew Henry
English author,
non-conformist minister
(1662-1714)

Reference verses:

Wherefore, as by one man sin entered into the world, and death by sin; and so death passed upon all men, for that all have sinned.

-Romans 5:12

Therefore do not let sin reign in your mortal body, that you should obey it in its lusts.

-Romans 6:12

John 8:34   Romans 5:20   Romans 6:17-23
James 1:14-15

Quote:

"Man is nothing but insincerity, falsehood, and hypocrisy, both in regard to others. He does not wish that he should be told the truth, he shuns saying it to others. And all these moods, so inconsistent with justice and reason, have their roots in his heart."

-Blaise Pascal,
French philosopher,

physicist, writer.
(1623-1662)

Commentary:

Sin is devastating, rampant and merciless. Sin is rebellion against a Holy God. Sin has placed a barrier between humanity and God that is impossible to cross without Divine intervention. Human sin is the cause of all problems on earth. It was stubborn human pride that allowed the curse of sin, and thus death, to enter creation and the human heart resulting in the Fall of Man. In the Garden of Eden, Adam (the first man), was appointed as the head of all humanity. His sinful rebellion against God abolished righteousness for all those he represented (Mankind). The Fall plunged us into corruption and we are now helpless to break free from the bondage of sin unless we seek the cure for this dark disease of the soul. The cure is Jesus Christ.

The word for sin in the Greek is *hamartia,* which means *"to miss the mark."* It is the picture of a person shooting a bow and arrow and missing their target. God has established His mark of righteousness for all men, and it is His view, His "target" of righteousness that must be upheld. God's standard is much higher than our feeble and sporadic human attempts at "being good." In the Old Testament, sin was also seen as a picture of breaking a covenant with someone. We see this in the covenantal relationship that God had with Israel through the Law and the sacrificial system. The breaking of this covenant in any way was seen by the Lord as sin against Him.

"For by the law is the knowledge of sin" (Romans 3:20b). The Law was given to insure that we would understand that perfection is impossible without God's grace, and that even the best of human efforts fall terribly short of God's standard for perfection (Exodus 20:1-17). We do not have the ability to keep the Law and this brings us to a place of guilt and the sobering realization of how profoundly

sinful we are. It is on the rock of the Law that we are broken. Our frailty and shame then points to the only hope we have for redemption, which is Jesus Christ. Until a person understands they are a sinner they cannot be saved because they will never seek redemption.

Romans chapter 3 reveals that all have fallen short of God's glory and we all bear the guilty stain of sin. To say that one is without sin is to call God a liar. The Bible is equally clear that sin did not originate with God, for He cannot sin or cause evil (I John 1:5). Satan, the wicked one, may tempt man to sin, but the reality is that sin originates in the rebellious heart of humanity. Jeremiah 17:9 states, *"The heart is deceitful above all things, and desperately wicked; who can know it?"*

Sin has deadened the human soul. This is why a seemingly normal "good" person can commit horrible acts against his family and fellow man. All the vile and bloody atrocities in our world stem from this brutal reality. Jesus states in Matthew chapter 15 that, *"...out of the heart proceed evil thoughts, murders, adulteries, fornication, thefts, false witnesses, blasphemies. These are the things that defile a man."* Apart from God there is no real goodness, grace or compassion.

The New Testament is clear that sin is the rejection of Jesus as the light of our salvation. It is the willful turning away from the standard of perfection, which is Christ. Unbelief is the rejection of Jesus as the revealed Son of God and *standard bearer* for humanity. This resistance to the truth of Christ produces spiritual darkness giving birth to sinful behavior and rebellious thinking. Sin must then be judged by the only One worthy to judge what sin really is, and that is God alone.

Sin always produces a harvest. Even as Christians we still struggle with the sin nature. We may get away with sinful behavior for a time but eventually there is a reckoning.

"Do not be deceived, God is not mocked; for what a man sows, that he will also reap" (Gal. 6:7). Sin always produces death: emotional, spiritual, and physical. We must be vigilant in our walk with Christ and living in the transforming power of His Spirit (Eph. 5:8). Only then can we daily be the living sacrifice He has called us to be (Rom.12:1-2). We also need to have a deeper sense of how much God despises sin. The best way to come to that realization is to see what it took to wash away the stain of man's sin: Only the brutal death and shedding of His righteous, perfect Son's blood could redeem us from the certain damnation our sin marked us for.

The ultimate punishment for sin is death and eternal separation from God. The willful rejection of God's gift of salvation through Christ leaves Him with only one option, and that is to put sin away from His eternal holiness. God cannot tolerate sin in any form. *"You shall be holy, for I the Lord your God, am holy"* (Lev. 19:2b). God is fair and just. If a person refuses to accept His standard for holiness (*which is Jesus*), God will then allow that person to stay in his sinfulness and be separated from Him forever in Hell.

We all have sinned against God and are powerless to stand as righteous before Him. The amazing truth is that we can be cleansed from the stain and penalty of sin. When we seek God's forgiveness with a repentant heart we are then reconciled to a Holy God through faith in the free gift of Jesus' grace and salvation. His righteousness is then imputed to us and we are now seen as righteous, no longer missing the mark, but safely redeemed by the grace, power and love of Christ!

Historical Figure: *Augustine of Hippo*

Augustine was the Bishop of Hippo, also known as Saint Augustine (354-430 AD). He was a brilliant philosopher and theologian. He is an important figure in the development of Western Christianity. He framed the concepts of the Trinity, original sin and just war. His theological thought profoundly influenced the medieval worldview and the theology of the Reformers. He continues to be a respected source for modern theologians.

Term: *"Subjectivism,"* the postmodern view that morality and truth are personal issues and there should be no outside objective standard. Example: what is morally true for one person or culture is not true for another.

Hymn: *"Amazing Grace"*
        Words: John Newton, 1779
        Music: Virginia Harmony, 1831

Amazing grace how sweet the sound
that saved a wretch like me,
I once was lost, but now I am found,
was blind but now I see.

The Trinity

Focus verse:

*F*or there are three that bear witness in Heaven; the Father, the Word, and the Holy Spirit; and these three are One.

-I John 5:7

Greek: The word *"trinity"* is not found in Scripture but the Trinitarian structure appears throughout the Word of God. Latin: *"Trinitas,"* meaning *"threeness."*

Theological note:
God is revealed to us as Father, Son and Holy Spirit each with distinct personal attributes, but without division of nature, essence, or being.

-Southern Baptist Theological Seminary, 1858

Pastoral quote:

"Tell me how in this room there are three candles and but one light, and I will explain to you the Trinity, the mode of the Divine existence."

-John Wesley

"The most excellent study for expanding the soul is the science of Christ and Him crucified and the knowledge of the Godhead in the glorious Trinity."
                                        -Charles Haddon Spurgeon

Reference verses:

But you are not in the flesh but in the Spirit, if indeed the Spirit of God dwells in you. Now if anyone does not have the Spirit of Christ he is not His.
                                                    -Romans 8:9

...elect according to the foreknowledge of God the Father, in sanctification of the Spirit, for obedience and sprinkling of the blood of Jesus Christ.
                                                    -I Peter 1:2

We are bound to give thanks to God always for you, Brethern beloved by the Lord, because God from the beginning chose you for salvation through sanctification by the Spirit and belief in the truth, to which He called you by our Gospel, for the obtaining of the glory of our Lord Jesus Christ.
                                        -II Thessalonians 2: 13-14

Matthew 28:19   Mark 1:9-10   John 17:9-11
Revelation 1:4-5

Quote:

"When we have said these three things, then, that there is but one God, that the Father and the Son and the Spirit is each God, that the Father and the Son and the Holy Spirit is each a distinct Person, we have enunciated the doctrine of the Trinity in it's completeness."

-Benjamin Breckinridge (B.B.) Warfield
Princeton Theologian
(1851-1921)

Commentary:

Trinity is the term we use to explain the Oneness of God. We worship the One true, living God. The Father, Son, and Holy Spirit are three distinct yet equal Persons and indivisibly One God. They are co-equal and co-eternal, each having the full divine essence of God. The Christian faith is a *monotheistic* faith meaning we serve and believe in only One God. This Oneness is a profound mystery but is clearly defined throughout Scripture. The Trinity is also called the *Godhead* as a term used to express the absolute authority, unity, and power of God.

The main errors in defining the Trinity are tritheism, and modalism. The tritheism view is that the Godhead breaks down into three distinct beings that are separate Gods. This is polytheism and is not what Scripture teaches. Modalism is the idea that God is one person but performs three different isolated roles. Again, this is contrary to the Bible.

The Latin word *Trinitas*, meaning *"threeness,"* first used by the theologian Tertullian (born A.D. 220), helps us put into words a concept that is humanly impossible to fully understand. The Trinity is a divine mystery and it is Biblical truth. The New Testament writers never contradict the Old Testament view of a monotheistic God. They all uphold the doctrine of God being *One*. This Trinitarian concept is revealed through Scripture, accepted in the early church, and was not seen as controversial.

The awesome truth is that God the Father, God the Son, and God the Holy Spirit are eternally One and equally participated in the redemption of Man.

"Holy, holy, holy is the Lord of hosts; the whole earth is full of His glory!"

-Isaiah 6:3

Historical Figure: *Irenaeus*

Saint Irenaeus was Bishop of Lugdunum in Gaul, then part of the Roman Empire. He was an early church father and apologist, and his writings were part of the early development of Christian theology. He was a student of Polycarp, who in turn was a student of the Apostle John. Irenaeus became one of the first great theologians of the Church. He promoted the idea of church unity by having one doctrinal authority. Irenaeus is the earliest to recognize the gospels were synoptic. His main ministry was defending the Christian faith against the Gnostics. His famous book was *"Against Heresies."* He was born AD c.115 and died AD c. 202.

Term: *"Pedagogic,"* pertaining to teaching, instruction and education.

Hymn: *"Holy, Holy, Holy"*
     Words: Reginald Heber, 1826
     Music: *"NICEA"*, John B. Dykes, 1861

Holy, Holy, Holy, Lord God Almighty,
early in the morning our song shall rise to Thee,
Holy, Holy, Holy, merciful and mighty,
God in three Persons, blessed Trinity.

Truth

Focus Verse:

*A*nd you shall know the Truth, and the Truth shall make you free.

-John 8:32

Greek: *Aletheia* (al-ayth-yoo'-o) true, truth, verity

Theological Note:
Truth is that which is reliable and can be trusted. The Bible uses truth in the general "factual" sense. Truth may designate the actual fact over against appearance, pretense, or assertion. Truth is correct doctrine or knowledge. God and His Word, the *Logos,* is the standard for all Truth because He is the ultimate authority of what is true or a falsehood. The *Logos* is all the truth that can be known.

Pastoral Quote:

"Nothing makes a man so virtuous as belief of the truth. A lying doctrine will beget a lying practice. A man cannot have an erroneous belief without by-and-by having an erroneous life. I believe the one thing naturally begets the other."

-C.H. Spurgeon

Reference Verses:

Jesus said to Him, "I am the Way, the Truth, and the Life. No one comes to the Father except through Me."

-John 14:6

That we should no longer be children, tossed to and fro and carried about by every wind of doctrine, by the trickery of men, in the cunning craftiness of deceitful plotting, but speaking the Truth in love, may grow up in all things into Him who is the Head, Christ.

-Ephesians 4:14-15

John 16:13   John 1:14   Romans 1:18   I Cor. 13:6
II Thess. 2:10

Quote:

"Truth is so obscure in these times, and falsehood so established, that, unless we love the truth, we cannot know it."

-Blaise Pascal

"I believe in Christianity as I believe that the sun has risen: not only because I see it, but because by it I see everything else."

-C.S. Lewis

Commentary:

What is *Truth*? This is the cry of our generation that is awash in relativism. How can we really know what is true? As Christians we have an answer to this profound question. *Jesus Christ is the Truth*. He is truth Personified. *"I am the Way, the Truth, and the Life..."* (John 14:6). *"And the Word (Logos) became flesh and dwelt among us"* (John 1:14). The truth of Christ is *true* in all places, people groups, time periods, and for eternity. This is why correct theology is vital in our generation. We are to know the Truth, for it is the Truth that sets us free (John 8:32). *God is Truth* and His truth is universal, unchanging, exclusive, and eternal. Only when we abide in His Word, the *Logos*, do we understand the verities of our Faith. *"Thy Word is a lamp unto my feet and a light unto my path"* (Ps. 119:105).

The Bible is clear that un-truth, falsehood, and lies originate with Satan and he constantly comes against the authority of God to bring people into deception and bondage. The devil's scheme to thwart the Word of God began in the Garden of Eden when he asked Eve, *"Has God indeed said...?"*(Gen. 3:1). He has continued the same assault on the authority of the Word throughout the centuries. We must stand against this attack and so know the Truth that we can spot a falsehood quickly and put it away from us. God's Word is our spiritual weapon against the Enemy and it is living, powerful and cannot fail (Ephesians chapter 6).

The Bible is God's truth revealed to man. This means we can find truth in the Word and then *put it into words*. It is not ethereal, strange, or vaguely mystical. Truth is not "secret knowledge" that only a few possess or mystically impart to others. It is never obtuse, chaotic, or just random "facts." The Truth of God is systematic and in full view. What we have in the structure of Christian doctrine simply contains the truths we have found in Scripture. That is why we should never seek what is *true* outside of the parameters of the Bible. We can certainly experience truth but we must be sure to anchor our experiences in the knowledge of the Word of God.

We should never avoid doctrine and theology in our spiritual quest for truth. We cannot fully understand truth apart from the study of the Bible. To avoid or ridicule doctrine is not only foolish, it is dangerous and devastating. Paul wrote to the Colossian church: *"As you therefore have received Christ Jesus the Lord, so walk in Him, rooted and built up in Him and established in the faith, as you have been taught, abounding in it with thanksgiving. Beware lest anyone cheat you through philosophy and empty deceit, according to the tradition of men, according to the basic principles of this world and not according to Christ"* (Col. 2:6-8).

The exclusive truth claims of the Bible will often contradict other religious or political systems, but we are to never compromise the Word of God in the name of being "politically correct" or tolerant of falsehood. When we compromise the Truth of Christ we quickly find ourselves being marginalized and unfruitful in our daily walk with Jesus. As dangerous as satanic deception is, we must realize that self-deception is just as brutal and seductive.

The book of *Jude* has severe warnings for false teachers. Why? Because it is through the teaching of the *true* Word of God, and the proclamation of the *true* Gospel, that people are saved and come into a righteous relationship with God through Jesus Christ. If false teachers twist the truth of the Bible and sway people to believe another gospel, or follow another "christ," they have in effect damned people to Hell for eternity. Truth matters.

We as Christians are to worship the Lord in Spirit and in Truth. We should always seek His truth and search the Scriptures as if searching for gold...something of immense value. Hiding Scripture in your heart through memory verses is a great way to build a solid foundation of truth for your life. Daily Scripture reading and prayer are vital to an intimate, dynamic walk with Christ. Ultimately we are to live out His Truth in our world, being ready to give an answer for the hope we have in us through Jesus Christ (I Peter 3:15).

"For I rejoiced greatly when brethren came and testified of the truth that is in you, just as you walk in the truth. I have no greater joy than to hear that my children walk in truth."

-III John: 3-4

Historical Figure: *George Whitefield*

Whitefield was born on December 16, 1714 in Gloucester, England. He was an Anglican minister who God used mightily as a catalyst for the *Great Awakening* in Great Britain and, especially, in the British North American colonies. He was a dynamic preacher and evangelist and had a great desire to bring the Gospel of Christ to common people outside of the Anglican Church assembly, even though his outreach was seen as controversial by the Anglican hierarchy. Whitefield's impact on modern day evangelism has been dramatic and inspiring. He died on September 30, 1770.

Term: *"Apostasy,"* the act of willfully falling away, forsaking, and abandoning the Christian faith by counterfeit believers/teachers.

Hymn: *"The Solid Rock"*
Words: Edward Mote, 1832
Music: William B. Bradbury, 1863

My hope is built on nothing less
than Jesus' blood and righteousness;
I dare not trust the sweetest frame,
but wholly lean on Jesus' name.
On Christ, the solid Rock, I stand;
all other ground is sinking sand,
all other ground is sinking sand.

Virgin Birth of Christ

Focus Verse:

T herefore the Lord Himself will give you a sign; Behold the virgin shall conceive and bear a Son and shall call His name Immanuel.

-Isaiah 7:14

Greek: *Parthenos* (par-then'-os) young maiden, unmarried daughter, a virgin

Theological Note:

Belief in the virgin birth of Jesus Christ is a central doctrine of historic Christian thought. The main point is the miraculous conception of Jesus and His Incarnation. There was no human father. This testifies to the fact of Jesus' deity and that He is the only begotten Son of God. The eternal righteousness and glory that Jesus had before the incarnation would not be tarnished by the bloodline of Adam's sin.

Pastoral Quote:

"Christ is the great central fact in the world's history. To Him, everything looks forward or backward, all the lines of history converge upon Him. All the great purposes

of God culminate in Him. The greatest and most momentous fact which the history of the world records is the fact of His birth.

-C.H. Spurgeon

Reference Verses:

Then the angel said to her, "Do not be afraid, Mary, for you have found favor with God. And behold, you will conceive in your womb and bring forth a Son, and shall call His name Jesus."

-Luke 1:30-31

Then Mary said to the angel, "How can this be, since I do not know a man?" And the angel said to her, "the Holy Spirit will come upon you, and the power of the Highest will overshadow you, therefore, also, that Holy one who is to be born will be called the Son of God."

-Luke 1:34-35

Matthew 1:23-24   Matthew 1:18

Quote:

"My soul magnifies the Lord, and my spirit has rejoiced in God my Savior. For He has regarded the lowly state of His maidservant; for behold henceforth all generations will call me blessed. For He who is mighty has done great things for me, and holy is His name."

-Mary, the mother of Jesus
the opening of the
"Magnificat" (Luke 1:46-49)

Commentary:

Scripture makes it clear that Joseph was not the father of Jesus and that Mary conceived through the power of God. The miraculous conception and birth of Jesus proves He was the Son of God. The conception of Jesus was not produced through some vulgar sexual act between a "god" and a human. It was a special act of God through the creative power of the Holy Spirit. This is the same creative concept of Genesis 1, where the Holy Spirit was present and active in the creation of the heavens and the earth. In Luke chapter 1 we see clearly that Jesus was conceived by the Holy Spirit to establish His qualifications to be the sinless Redeemer and Savior of the world.

The Incarnation of Jesus Christ insured that His blood would not be tainted by the sinful blood of Adam, the first man. Jesus is then raised as the legal (adopted) son of Joseph that also established Jesus' lineage to King David's throne. The virgin birth of Christ was rarely questioned until the 19th century as *modernism* cast doubt on all miracles found in the Bible.

The virgin birth of Jesus Christ is a primary doctrine of the Christian faith. This is a non-negotiable doctrinal stand if one is to truly claim to be a follower of Christ. There will always be a vicious attack on this teaching because of its fundamental premise: *Jesus is the Son of God*. It means Jesus was much more than just a good teacher or "holy man" who started a religious movement. It means that the infinite became incarnate (flesh) and remained sinless.

The theological term for this is called the *hypostatic union*. This doctrine states that Jesus was not 50% man and 50% God, or some other hybrid formation, but that Jesus, the eternal Son of God became a man. Fully man, fully God. In doing so He retained His Godly nature but would forevermore exist in human form. The Bible teaches that Jesus now sits at the right hand of the Father in Heaven in His resurrected, glorified body.

What this doctrine teaches is that Jesus Christ is God and there is no one like Him. It means that when He spoke, He spoke the Word of God. It means that His death on the cross actually paid the price for man's sin and that we are all accountable to Him. It means that Bible prophecy is 100% true which means the whole of the Bible is true. It firmly states to all of mankind that Jesus is the only way to Heaven because He alone, as God, had the power to conquer the grave. It also clearly means that all other religious systems and cults are false and lead to eternal destruction.

The stark reality of the virgin birth of Christ is that the Son of God entered into the frailty of human suffering at an appointed time in history. He would be the God we could know, see, touch, walk beside, and speak with. He came to be our High Priest who could sympathize with our weaknesses and temptations and yet remain the sinless Savior.

Jesus' sinless nature was necessary because only then could He fulfill the righteous requirements to be the spotless Lamb of God who would take away the sin of the world. By shedding His precious blood on the cross Jesus made a way for all those who will believe on Him to be a part of His righteous, glorious, eternal Kingdom.

"And behold, you will conceive in your womb and bring forth a Son, and shall call His name JESUS. He will be great, and will be called the Son of the Highest; and the Lord God will give Him the throne of His father David. And He will reign over the house of Jacob forever, and His kingdom there will be no end."

-Luke 1:31-33

Historical Figure: *George Fox*

George Fox (1624-1691) was born in Leicestershire to Puritan parents. He began his spiritual journey with Christ at 18 years of age and had a deep desire to follow Jesus in purity and obedience. He realized early that the Church of England was a detriment to people hearing the Gospel, so he began a traveling preaching ministry in 1647. His ministry brought people the truth of how Christ is available to all people without professional help from clergy. His "Inner Light" teaching proclaimed that only Jesus could heal the broken heart of man and Jesus responded to people individually. He was imprisoned for his stand against the Church of England and while in court he warned the judge, "*to tremble at the Word of God.*" This statement earned him and his followers the name of "Quakers" which became a denomination that still exists today. Fox was persecuted and imprisoned several more times and eventually did mission work in North America and the West Indies. He was imprisoned again on his return to London and then spent the rest of his life building the Quaker church.

Term: *"Incarnation,"* God becoming flesh. The union of divinity and humanity. Jesus Christ, God incarnate, one Person with two natures, fully divine and fully human.

Hymn: *"Silent Night"*
        Words: German Hymn, Joseph Mohr, 1818, translated 1863 by John F. Young.
        Music: Stille Nacht, Franz Gruber, 1818

Silent Night, Holy Night,
All is calm, All is bright,
Round yon virgin, mother and child,
Holy infant so tender and mild,
Sleep in heavenly peace,
Sleep in heavenly peace.

Worship

Focus Verse:

*G**reat** and marvelous are Your works, Lord God Almighty! Just and true are Your ways, O King of the Saints! Who shall not fear You, O Lord, and glorify Your name? For You alone are holy. For all nations shall come and worship before You, for Your judgments have been manifested.*

-Revelation 15: 3-4

Greek: *Proskuneo* (pros-koo-neh'-o) to worship, to prostrate oneself in homage, to adore

Theological Note:

Religious worship is to be given to God, the Father, Son, Holy Ghost; and to Him alone, not to angels, saints, or any other creature; and since the Fall, not without a Mediator; nor in the mediation of any other but of Christ alone.

-Westminster Confession 1646

Pastoral Quote:

"There is nothing in the world worth living for but doing good and finishing God's work, doing the work that

Christ did. I see nothing else in the world that can yield any satisfaction besides living for God, pleasing Him and doing His whole will."

-David Brainerd
American missionary
to Native Americans
(1718-1747)

Reference verses:

O come, let us worship and bow down, Let us kneel before the Lord our Maker. For He is our God, and we are the people of His pasture, and the sheep of His Hand.

-Psalm 95: 6-7

Stand up and bless the Lord your God forever and ever! Blessed be Your glorious name, which is exalted above all blessing and praise! You alone are the Lord: You have made Heaven, the Heaven of heavens with all their host, the earth and everything on it, and the seas and all that is in them. And You preserve them all. The host of Heaven worships You.

-Nehemiah 9:5-6

Exodus 20:3   Hebrews 1:5-8   John 9:31
Matthew 28:9

Quote:

"A man can no more diminish God's glory by refusing to worship Him than a lunatic can put out the sun by scribbling the word, 'darkness' on the walls of His cell."

–C.S. Lewis

Commentary:

The word *"worship"* is derived from *"worth-ship,"* which means *to ascribe worth to someone or something.* Jesus said that true worshippers would worship the Father in spirit and in truth (John 4:23). This is the key aspect of worship...we must worship only the one true living God. All other worship is vain, senseless, and dangerous. True worship is not about styles of music or orders of service. It is not restricted to certain cultures, places, times, or rituals. Worship of God is our free response to His majesty, righteousness, holiness, and graciousness.

Worship can be intensely personal or a celebratory occasion with other believers. Singing, prayer, silence, testimony, giving, baptism, communion, preaching, and the reading of the Word can all be acts of worship. The main thing is that our motives are pure, Christ is exalted, and God is glorified in every occasion. God does not exist to make you happy. You exist to worship Him and honor Him with your life.

Worship should always pour out from a heart overflowing with thankfulness and awe. When we get a glimpse of Heaven in Scripture we see a place that is full of praise, wonder and awe as the Heavenly hosts worship Almighty God! We are to participate in worship. It is not for spectators. Can it touch your emotions? Certain acts of worship will move our emotions but not always. Believers express their worship of God in many different ways because of our various personalities, but the key aspect of all worship is that Jesus Christ is the focus; not a worship leader, music group, pastor, or other human participants.

It is interesting in our modern day churches that many believers seem to have lost the ability to simply be still and hear God's voice. We feel that a "praise and worship service" has to be full of activity, production and music. Do not neglect inner reflection (honestly assessing our motives), meditation (concentrating on the truth and promises of specific Scripture), prayer, and the mystery and awe of God's very presence in the life of all believers.

Let nothing get in the way of worshiping Jesus Christ... not even your guilt and sin. When we have sinned and feel so distant from God we can come to the Throne and ask for forgiveness. As the Holy Spirit brings conviction and draws us near to Christ, we, with a repentant heart, then begin to worship God. Jesus can bring beauty out of ashes. How amazing that any one of us, no matter what we have done, can be restored and become true worshipers of Almighty God.

During the 19th century it was popular for Christians to sign their letters to each other with the initials *"SDG"* below their name. This was an abbreviation of the Latin phrase *"Sola Deo Gloria,"* meaning *"To the Glory of God alone."* In the truest sense this should be the response of our hearts toward the Lord Jesus. We worship because of our love for Him, and that He alone be glorified. We worship Jesus with love and awe because we realize He first loved us, and He alone is worthy of all devotion and honor!

"He (Jesus) is the image of the invisible God, the first-born over all creation. For by Him all things were created that are in heaven and that are on earth, visible and invisible, whether thrones or dominions or principalities or powers. All things were created through Him and for Him. And He is before all things, and in Him all things consist. And He is the Head of the body, the church, who is the beginning, the firstborn from the dead, that in all things He may have the preeminence."

-Colossians 1:15-18

Historical Figure: *C.H. Spurgeon*

Charles Hadden (C.H.) Spurgeon was born in Kelveden, Essex on June 19, 1834. He was a British theologian and Baptist minister, still known today as the "Prince of Preachers." He preached up to ten times a week and proclaimed the Word to approximately 10 million people in his lifetime. He is one of the most quoted pastors in history and his influence on pastoral preaching, orthodox theology, and evangelism is enormous and far-reaching. He died on January 31, 1892.

Term: *"Monotheism,"* system of religious belief that says only one God exists. Christianity is a monotheistic faith.

Hymn: *"To God be the Glory"*
        Words: Fanny J. Crosby, 1875
        Music: William H. Doane, 1875

To God be the glory, great things He hath done;
so loved He the world that He gave us His Son,
who yielded His life an atonement for sin,
and opened the life-gate that all may go in.
Praise the Lord, praise the Lord, Let the earth
hear His voice! Praise the Lord, praise the Lord,
let the people rejoice! O come to the Father,
thro' Jesus the Son, and give Him the glory,
great things He hath done. Amen.

Items of Interest

The 5 primary doctrines of the Christian Faith

1. The Virgin Birth/Deity of Jesus Christ.
2. The Second Coming of Christ.
3. The Bodily resurrection of Christ.
4. Sacrificial blood atonement of Christ.
5. The Bible is the authoritative Word of God.

These core doctrines have been upheld by the historical Christian Church in defining the accepted, foundational beliefs that identify the true follower of Jesus Christ.

The six divisions of the Old Testament:

1. *The Law* (Genesis-Deuteronomy)
2. *Historical* (Joshua-Esther)
3. *Wisdom* (Job-Proverbs)
4. *Poetic* (Ecclesiastes & Song of Solomon)
5. *Prophets:* Major: Isaiah-Daniel
   Minor: Hosea-Micah
6. *Intertestamental Period*: the 400 year period between *Old Testament* writings and *New Testament* writings. (The *Apocrypha* writings were penned during this period.)

The Ten Commandments

Exodus Chapter 20

I. You shall have no other gods before Me.
II. You shall not make for yourself a carved image, any likeness of anything that is in heaven above, or that is in the earth beneath, or that is in the water under the earth.
III. You shall not take the name of the LORD your God in vain.
IV. Remember the Sabbath day, to keep it holy.
V. Honor your father and your mother.
VI. You shall not murder.
VII. You shall not commit adultery.
VIII. You shall not steal.
IX. You shall not bear false witness against your neighbor.
X. You shall not covet your neighbor's house; you shall not covet your neighbor's wife, nor his male servant, nor his female servant, nor his ox, nor his donkey, nor anything that is your neighbor's.

1,400 years later Jesus summed up the *Ten Commandments* when He was challenged by the religious leaders of the day:

"Teacher, which is the greatest commandment in the Law?" Jesus replied: 'Love the Lord your God with all your heart and with all your soul and with all your mind.' This is the first and greatest commandment. And the second is like it: 'Love your neighbor as yourself.' All the Law and the Prophets hang on these two commandments.
-Matthew 22:36-40

The Apocrypha: the word means "hidden" or "secret." These books were written during the Intertestamental Period. Many

Jews gave much weight to these books. The Apocrypha was included in the *Septuagint*, the Greek translation of the Old Testament. It was also included in the original printing of the 1611 *King James* Bible. Palestinian Jews rejected these books as inspired Scripture. Roman Catholics at the Council of Trent (AD 1546) declared 11 of the books to be Holy Writ. The overall view of the *Apocrypha* by the early church fathers and subsequent church leadership in the past many centuries is that these books have *historical merit* but their *canonicity* is rejected. They are deemed as *not* inspired by the Holy Spirit and should not be included with the accepted 66 authoritative books of the Bible as Holy Scripture.

Books of the Apocrypha:

I Esdras, II Esdras, Tobit, Judith, Additions to Esther, The Wisdom of Solomon, Ecclsiaticus, The Epistle of Jeremiah, The Song of the Three Holy Children, The History of Susanna, Bel and the Dragon, The Prayer of Manasses, I & II Maccabees, III & IV Maccabees.

The 4 criteria for *exclusion* of any Old Testament era writing is as follows:

1. It was never quoted by Christ.
2. Early Church Father's disputed them.
3. They did not appear in the ancient Hebrew Canon.
4. They are of inferior writing quality.

4 main attacks against the Bible in the past 100 years:

1. *Liberalism:* doubting the veracity of the *authorship* of each book.
2. *Neo-orthodoxy:* questioning the accuracy of the Bible regarding *historical facts and archeology.*
3. *Relevancy:* It is old and *out of touch* with modern society and theological systems.

4. *Sufficiency:* The Word we have *is not enough.* We need more, deeper truth.

These attacks are from false teachers, apostates, and hostile unbelievers attempting to subvert the eternal truth of God's Word.

"Let God be true, and every man a liar." -Romans 3:4

Timeline of Major Bible Translations Throughout History:

*Approximately 1400 B.C. The first written Word of God is the *Ten Commandments* delivered to Moses at Mount Sinai by God Himself. (Exodus 20)

*500 B.C.: Completion of all original Hebrew manuscripts by Old Testament Prophets and Authors painstakingly transcribed by the *Jewish Scribes* which make up the 39 Books of the Old Testament.

*By the 6th century A.D. this task was given to the *Masoretes* who preserved the sacred text for another 500 years in a form called the *Masoretic Text.* By the 10th century the family of *ben Asher* took on that duty. By the 12th century theirs was the only recognized form of the Hebrew Scriptures.

(In 1524 Jacob ben Chayyim published the first Hebrew text. It was used by the King James translators. It was also used in the *Biblia Hebraica* of 1906.)

The Dead Sea Scrolls are Old Testament manuscripts dated to 100 B.C. and 70 A.D. They were discovered in a cave near Qumran on the Dead Sea between 1947 and 1960. They are manuscript copies produced by a Jewish sect known as the *Essenes.*

* 200 B.C.: The *Septuagint,* aka: *LXX* (Roman numeral *seventy,* the tradition being that *70* scholars put this Bible together) the Greek translation of the Old Testament.

* First century A.D. Completion of all original Greek manuscripts which make up all the 27 New Testament Books.

*A.D. 382: Jerome's *Latin Vulgate* manuscripts containing the 66 Books of the Bible and the 14 books of the *Apocrypha*. (A.D. 600: Latin declared the only language permitted for Scripture by the Roman Catholic Church. This was the beginning of the *"Dark Ages."*)

*A.D. 1382: *The Wycliffe Bible*: John Wycliffe produces the first English language Bible. Hand-written 200 years before the *Reformation Period*.

*A.D. 1455: Gutenberg invents the printing press. The first book ever printed was the *Gutenberg Bible* in Latin.

*A.D. 1516: *Erasmus* produces a Greek/Latin parallel New Testament using a compilation of Greek OT and NT manuscripts called the *Textus Receptus,* (*"Received Text"*).

*A.D. 1522: *Martin Luther's* German New Testament.

*A.D. 1526: *William Tyndale's* English New Testament.

*A.D. 1535: *Myles Coverdale's Bible*: The first complete English Bible.

*A.D. 1537: *Tyndale-Matthews Bible*: second complete English Bible.

*A.D. 1539: *"The Great Bible"*: The first English Bible authorized for public use.

*A.D. 1560: *The Geneva Bible*: The first English Bible to add numbered verses to each chapter. (This was the Bible Shakespeare used, and the Bible the Puritans and Pilgrims brought to America.)

*A.D. 1568: *The Bishop's Bible*: The Bible of which the King James was a revision (included the Apocrypha.)

*A.D. 1609: *The Douay Old Testament* is added to the Reims New Testament (1582) making the first English Catholic Bible. Translated from the Latin and including the *Apocrypha*.

*A.D. 1611: *The King James Bible*: revised from the *Bishop's Bible* and much of Tyndale's early work. Included the *Apocrypha*. In 1885 the *Apocrypha* was removed from this version of the Bible. (More copies sold of this translation than any other, over 1 billion copies since it was introduced.) *(Since *1769* the King James Version Bibles printed in America use the *Baskerville* spelling and wording revision of the 1611. The only way to obtain an original, unaltered *KJV* is to find a pre-1769 copy or a reproduction of the actual 1611 Bible.)

*A.D. 1663: first Bible printed in America was in the *Algonquin Indian Language* by John Eliot.

*A.D. 1841: The English *Hexapla* New Testament. Comparison of the Greek and six English translations in parallel columns.

*A.D. 1881: *The English Revised Version.*

*A.D. 1901: *The American Standard Version.* Major revision of the *KJV*.

*A.D. 1971: *The New American Standard Bible*: modern translation using the principle of "formal equivalence."

*A.D. 1973: *The New International Version*: modern translation using the principle of "dynamic equivalency."

*A.D. 1982: *The New King James Version*: modern revision of the *KJV.*

*A.D. 2002: *The English Standard Version*: published to bridge the gap between the readability of the *NIV* and the accuracy of the *NASB*.

One of the main goals of the leaders of the **Protestant Reformation** was to get the *Word of God* into the hands of common people. The light of the Reformation was the illumination of the Bible. No longer was it to be hidden in an ancient language no one could read, but now translated into everyday language for all to understand and embrace.

William Tyndale fought and died for the right to print the Bible in the English of his day. When criticized by a Roman Catholic Official for attempting to translate the Bible for all

English speaking people Tyndale proclaimed, *"If God spare my life, I will see to it that the boy who drives the plowshare knows more of Scripture than you, Sir!"* He was burned at the stake in 1536, but only after he accomplished his mission.

It is our duty now to preserve the written *Word of God* for future generations and to make sure they understand it in modern, accurate translations in all nations and languages. We do not worship the *Bible*, we worship the God of the Bible who gave us His Word in written form through human agents inspired by the Holy Spirit. May we be diligent in maintaining Scriptural integrity by always comparing modern translations with the earliest ancient Hebrew and Greek manuscripts that are copies of the original inerrant and infallible scriptures.

You can trust God's Word and confidently build your life on the Truth found inside its covers.

Study Bible recommendations:

The Life Application Bible, The New Geneva Study Bible, Thompson Chain Reference Bible, Greek-Hebrew Key Study Bible, Dake Annotated Study Bible, Ryrie Study Bible
(These are great study Bibles and most come in the KJV, NKJV, NIV and NASB.)

Definitions:

Jesus: Greek form of the Hebrew name *Joshua*, meaning *"Yahweh is Salvation."*

Yahweh: Hebrew name for God. Also, *Yah,* in the shortened form. (*YHWH*)

Jehovah: English transliteration of the Hebrew divine name, *Yahweh.*

El: *God*

Immanuel: *"God with us"*

Christ: *"The Anointed One."* From the Greek, *"Christos."*

Messiah: Transliteration of the Hebrew word meaning, *"Anointed One."*
Adoni: *"Lord"*
Hallelujah: *"Praise Yahweh!"*
Hosanna: *"Save, I beseech You!"* A cry of praise and adoration to God.
Amen: *"So be it."* Signifying something is certain, true, faithful or sure.

The twelve original disciples:
(Matthew 10:2-4, Mark 3:16-19, Luke 6:13-16, Acts 1:13-14)

1. Simon Peter
2. Andrew
3. James, son of Zebedee
4. John
5. Philip
6. Bartholomew
7. Thomas
8. Matthew the publican
9. James, son of Alphaeus
10. Thaddeus (Lebbeus)
11. Simon the Canaanite
12. Judas Iscariot

(Matthias later replaced Judas.)

Fruit of The Holy Spirit: Galatians 5:22-23
Love, Joy, Peace, Longsuffering, Kindness, Goodness, Faithfulness, Gentleness,
Self-control.

The appearances of the Resurrected Lord Jesus:

- At the empty tomb outside of Jerusalem (Matthew 28:1-10)
- To Mary Magdalene at the tomb (Mark 16:9-11)
- To the Two travelers on the road to Emmaus (Luke 24:13-32)
- To Peter in Jerusalem (Luke 24:34)
- To the ten disciples in the upper room (John 20:19-25)
- To the eleven disciples in the upper room (John 20:26-31)
- To the seven disciples fishing on the Sea of Galilee (John 21:1-23)
- To the eleven disciples on the mountain in Galilee (Matthew 28:16-20)
- To more than 500 people (I Corinthians 15:6)
- To James (I Corinthians 15:7)
- At Jesus' Ascension on the Mount of Olives (Luke 24:44-49)
- To Paul (I Corinthians 15:8)

The Apostle's Creed

I believe in God the Father almighty maker of heaven and earth; and in Jesus Christ His only Son our Lord, who was conceived by the Holy Ghost; born of the Virgin Mary; suffered under Pontius Pilate; was crucified, dead and buried; He descended into hell (Hades); the third day He rose again from the dead, he ascended into Heaven, and sitteth on the right hand of God the Father almighty, from thence He shall come to judge the quick and the dead. I believe in the Holy Ghost, the holy catholic (universal) church, the communion of saints, the forgiveness of sins, the resurrection of the body, and the life everlasting. Amen.

"The Apostle's Creed, so called. This Creed gradually grew out of the comparison and assimilation of the Baptismal Creeds of the principle Churches in the West and Latin half of the ancient Church. The most complete and popular forms of these baptismal creeds were those of Rome, Aquileja, Milan, Ravenna, Carthage, and Hippo...it was subjoined by the Westminster divines to their Catechism, together with the Lord's Prayer and the Ten Commandments not as though it was composed by the apostles or ought to be esteemed canonical scripture, but because it is a brief sum of Christianity agreeable to the Word of God and anciently received in the Churches of Christ...for the purpose of preservation and of popular instruction, of discriminating and defending the truth from perversion of heretics and the attacks of infidels, and affording a common bond of faith and rule of teaching and discipline."

A.A. Hodge (1823-1886)
"Outlines of Theology" 1860

Other Notable Creeds of the Early Church

The Nicene Creed
Ecumenical Council of Nice, A.D. 325
(The Trinity is defined and established as church doctrine.)

The Athanasian Creed
Modern scholars trace this creed to North Africa and the school of Augustine, not Athanasius, the Bishop of Alexandria, 328 A.D. The complete form does not appear until the 8th century A.D.

The Creed of Chalcedon
The Emperor Marcianus called the fourth ecumenical council to meet in Chalcedon in Bithynia to put down the Eutychian and Nestorian heresies. The council consisted of 630 Bishops.

The Didache
"Teaching of the Twelve Apostles"
Not a Creed, but an ancient Christian *church manual* which was used extensively in the early church to help the daily functioning of local fellowships stay true to the Apostles teachings. It was rediscovered in 1883. It consists of orthodox instruction on matters of the church such as baptism, communion, fasting, prayer, hospitality, worship on the Lord's Day, bishops and deacons. Probably originated in Syria.
It is dated to 150 A.D. or earlier.

Hymn History:
I have placed at the end of each theological subject a portion of the lyrics to some of the great hymns of the Faith. I did this to showcase and acknowledge the poetry and orthodox doctrine of these songs and the important place that hymn writing and singing has held in Church history.

Martin Luther once said, *"After theology, there is nothing that can be placed on a level with music. It drives out the devil and makes people cheerful. It is a gift that God gave to birds and men. We need to remove hymn singing from the domain of monks and priests and set the laity (congregation) to singing. By the singing of hymns the laity can publicly express their love to the Almighty God."*

Luther's most famous hymn, *"A Mighty Fortress Is Our God,"* was inspired by Psalm 46 and was the battle cry of the Reformation Period. The Church throughout history, from

King David, to Bach, to modern Christian songwriters, has produced the most beautiful music on earth. God has used that music powerfully to proclaim the Gospel to the world and to encourage the heart of the believer.

Recommended authors and Bible teachers:

Ravi Zacharias, Lee Strobel, Josh McDowell, Steve Brown, Elizabeth Elliott, R.C. Sproul, Philip Yancey, Greg Laurie, Charles Swindoll, Philip E. Johnson, C.H. Spurgeon, C.S. Lewis, A.W. Tozer, William Lane Craig, Francis Schaeffer, Warren Wiersbe, Kay Arthur, J. Vernon McGee, Adrian Rogers, David Jeremiah, James MacDonald, Billy Graham, H.A. Ironside, Henry Blackaby.

Recommended devotionals:
* *My Utmost For His Highest,* Oswald Chambers
* *Experiencing God,* daily devotional, Henry Blackaby
* *The One Year Bible,* read through the entire Bible in 12 months.
* *The Book of Proverbs*
* *The Book of Psalms*
*Start a *Prayer and Scripture Journal*: read through books of the Bible line by line, chapter by chapter. Take notes of key verses, Scriptural insights, and daily log how many books and chapters covered in a month/year. Also use it to write down prayer requests, answered prayers, spiritual milestones, etc.

An Invitation:

*I*f you have not yet received Jesus as your Savior please invite Him into your heart today!
Jesus loves you and He is the only way to Heaven. Romans 10:13 says that, *"Whoever calls upon the name of the Lord will be saved."* How do you do this? First admit you are a sinner and need forgiveness. Repent of your sin, turning to Christ alone. Believe that Jesus shed His blood on the cross and died for your redemption, that He was buried, and on the third day God raised Him from the dead. Now by faith, in accordance to His Word, accept Jesus as your Lord and Savior.

Prayer:

Lord Jesus, thank you for Your great love and sacrifice. I put my faith in You alone for my salvation. In You I am made righteous before God and complete. I repent of all my sin and ask You to forgive me and wash me clean. I believe that You are the risen Lord. Thank you for saving me and for everlasting life. I love You and I will serve You with all of my heart and life. Help me to stand on Your Word and grow in Your grace and knowledge. In the name of Jesus Christ I pray, Amen.

If you received Jesus as your Lord and Savior please let us know. *CPM* will send you discipleship materials that will help as you begin your new journey with Jesus Christ. Also let us know if you need a Bible or help finding a Christ-centered church in your area. Ministry contact info at: **www. christpoweredministries.com**

CPSIA information can be obtained at www.ICGtesting.com
Printed in the USA
239668LV00003B/4/P